A Grown-up's Guide to Guinea Pigs

A Grown-up's Guide to Guinea Pigs

Dale L. Sigler

Writer's Showcase
presented by *Writer's Digest*
San Jose New York Lincoln Shanghai

A Grown-up's Guide to Guinea Pigs

Writer's Showcase
presented by *Writer's Digest*
an imprint of iUniverse.com, Inc.

For information address:
iUniverse.com, Inc.
5220 S 16th, Ste. 200
Lincoln, NE 68512
www.iuniverse.com

Medical information contained in this book is for advice purposes only, you should always consult a competent exotics veterinarian when your guinea pig is sick. Any errors in information are the author's fault, every effort was made to check with reliable sources.

ISBN: 0-595-14194-3

Printed in the United States of America

Dedication

This book is dedicated to Honeybear, a darling Golden Agouti sow who taught me much more then I ever expected about love and loss. Hopefully this book will help others not to make the mistakes that I did with her, and that their guinea pig will be as forgiving as she was of me.

Contents

What is a Guinea Pig?

Housing

Diet

Handling

Behavior

Grooming

Health

Senior Citizens

Cage

Bedding

Food Dish

Water Source

Hay Rack

Salt Lick

Hideout

Cleaning the Habitat

Pellets

Water

Hay

List of Illustrations

List of Tables

Preface

Authors are often asked why they have written a book. In this case, the answer is easy—because it needed to be written! I have read numerous books about guinea pigs and belong to several on-line communities, many of which are familiar with the same titles. With the exception of Peter Gurney's books, most of the books lack critical information. Many of the publications are written for children who are getting a guinea pig for a pet, not for the adults who end up caring for the pet once the children lose interest. I've often seen the first posting in an on-line group from such an adult, with panic in their message, asking how to care for these little creatures.

I became familiar with guinea pigs as an adult. The first guinea pig entered my life when my oldest daughter got engaged to a gentleman who had stray cats as pets. So as a result, I inherited her two guinea pigs "temporarily." I quickly discovered that these animals, when given the opportunity, could be as interesting as any dog or cat, but in far more subtle ways. Their gentle nature and small size make them ideal as cuddly, huggable companions.

After Manda Mae and Spazz came to live with me and my family—and we found what a joy they could be—we purchased our next guinea pig from a pet store. Honeybear came to us with torn ears, a timid demeanor and decidedly pregnant. Starting from that time, I became an avid researcher on the care of these little animals. I wanted to ensure that Honeybear had a safe delivery and that we would provide the proper care for her babies. A few days before Valentine's Day, she delivered four healthy babies, or so we thought. Since then we've had a constant and often losing battle for the welfare of these little ones.

During this time we learned a lot about guinea pigs, and about good and bad methods for breeding these animals and also about rescue groups. Right now, with the exception of one of Honeybear's boys, all of our guinea pigs are rescues. The herd that lives in our home currently numbers eight–having lost four in the last few months to old age and disease–and is generally referred to as the Marauding Horde!

Based on these experiences, I am hoping that this slim volume will provide adults with the basic information needed to ensure that the guinea pigs in their care lead long and healthy lives. I also hope that people will come to understand why I am such a strong advocate of rescue and would like to see the veterinary profession expand its awareness and training in the care of guinea pigs.

I am also willing to continue to learn and I would appreciate any feedback from the reader. I can be contacted at CTCavyCare@AOL.COM. I am always willing to answer questions on-line and accept constructive criticism regarding this book and its contents. My purpose is not to become rich and famous, but to ensure that guinea pigs live the best possible lives.

Dale Sigler

Acknowledgements

No book is ever written in a vacuum. This one is based on the inputs and support of many people.

First of all, I would like to thank Penny Christopher for giving me unvarnished advice on the content for this book. A friend who tells you what you need to hear is a valuable asset indeed. Without her input, this book would not be as complete as it is. Thanks Penny.

Dr. Eva Ceranowicz reviewed the medical chapter, and, I suspect, got a chance to learn some things herself while helping me to learn some things as well. Thanks Doc, for taking time from your busy practice to review the materials.

My wife and daughters have supported this effort from the very beginning and offered a great deal of encouragement. I've been able to do something that I never dreamed I would do—write a book.

And then there is the on-line community of guinea pig lovers out there. This community is an interesting group of people from the ACBA breeders who work so hard at producing a better cavy to the hard-core rescuers who often have more pigs than they ever dreamed they could manage. They have all contributed to this work by providing sound advice and questions. Without their existence, I never would have thought that this book needed to be written in the first place. My first efforts involved creating a website with important information about guinea pigs, but then I realized that many "guinea pig" people are not on-line. I have written this book with them in mind and hope they will find something of value in it.

Caviae amor omnia vincit
Dale Sigler

Introduction

So here you are, an adult human with this little guinea pig in your hand. You're not sure how it got there and you're not sure what to do with it. Either you inherited it from a child who has lost interest or can't or won't keep it for some other reason or you remembered having one as a child and wanted to have a guinea pig as a pet. But now what?

First of all, you are not crazy. Many adults are very fond of guinea pigs or cavies. In fact, many adults lead perfectly normal lives away from the darlings, but are totally enthralled by them when at home. Some adults have been secret admirers for many years and think they are the only grown-ups who love these little creatures. Some adults are crazy enough not only to love them, but also to breed and show them. Others are crazy enough to become rescuers and keep cavies safe until a new home can be found. Many adults become very attached to guinea pigs and grieve for them when they're gone.

This book is written for the adults who feel like they have entered an entirely new world. Like me, you may have had dogs or cats when you were younger or may own one now. In any case, you have a guinea pig now and are wondering what to do with it to ensure that it has a long and enjoyable life.

I hope that I can provide you with enough information or at least point you to other resources that will help you ensure your guinea pig's well-being. The darling creatures have captured my heart and are a great joy to have around, even when the occasional sickness strikes or when that inevitable day of passing comes. I hope that some of my joy and love will come through in this book.

When possible, I'll try to provide definitive answers. However, if this isn't possible, then I will try to offer several alternatives. Do not be surprised if I make editorial comments along the way! I will base many of my comments on my own experiences with a fair-sized herd of guinea pigs (referred to as the Marauding Horde!), conversations with breeders, rescuers and other fanciers and other books that I have read. Since I also belong to several on-line communities, where conversations and "debates" on certain topics rage, I will incorporate that information in this guide as well. Additional information about these resources will be included in the Resource Listing.

I will provide a "Quick Start" in Chapter One and then expand each area in the following chapters. These chapters will cover topics such as identifying a healthy guinea pig, housing and bedding, providing proper food and water, general behavior and sounds, health issues and how guinea pigs can live in harmony with other pets. These sections should address the most commonly asked questions that crop up for new guinea pig owners. Naturally, everything written here is my opinion. However, when it isn't my opinion, I will identify the source of the information. Hopefully, everything you read will help you keep your little darling happy and healthy!

Dale and the Marauding Horde!
Bloomfield CT

Chapter One

Quick Start

What Is a Guinea Pig?

The guinea pig or "cavy" is currently considered a rodent, although there is some indication that this classification may not be totally true. The rabbit has been removed from the rodent class, and it looks like the cavy may soon join it as a separate species. The cavy is a herbivore. It has a digestive system designed to breakdown cellulose and use it as food.

The guinea pig is usually about a foot long when it reaches full adult size. It has four toes on each front foot and three toes on each rear foot. The normal adult weighs approximately two to four pounds, which may vary from breed to breed. It has a light skeleton, can move very quickly in forward and

reverse directions and can make a right turn at near full speed. It has continuously growing teeth. Like the rabbit and beaver, these teeth allow it to eat the hard vegetation that is the staple of its diet.

The most common variety of guinea pig, called the American, has a shorthaired coat that conforms closely to the body. This breed comes in a wide range of colors from white to black and many colors in between. In addition the American can come in a variety of Agoutis. These cavies have hair shafts with three different colors in them, giving the animal a ticked look that is very attractive.

Cavies make several sounds—most of which do not require them to open their mouths. They also flap their ears while they whistle. They have a split upper lip that gives them a bit of a buck-toothed appearance. There are thirteen breeds of guinea pigs recognized by the American Cavy Breeders Association (ACBA). Appendix A contains a listing of the currently recognized breeds. Additional breeds are recognized in Europe and Australia. These breeds may eventually find their way to the Americas.

Guinea pigs are active at all times of the day and night, unlike many other small mammals that are nocturnal. They seem to operate on many short naps, rather than one long sleep period. They also do not display any hibernation related habits, but remain active year round. Some people have noticed, especially in guinea pigs that rely mostly on natural light, that their animals are very active at dusk. This is the time when most birds settle down for the night and wouldn't be hunting small animals for food.

Housing

The preferred housing for guinea pigs includes a cage with a solid floor and wire sides. Cavies need a solid surface to walk on. The floor can be covered with newspaper and a bedding material. Acceptable bedding materials include: Kiln-dried pine, aspen or other hardwood materials, *CareFresh* or other paper products (waste or recycled). Cedar should never be used! The aromatic hydrocarbons in the cedar cause a guinea pig's liver to operate improperly. This failure can lead to general system dysfunction and death. In addition, cedar is considered a common cause of respiratory and allergic problems in small animals. So stay away from cedar.

A wire-walled cage gives good air circulation, protection from other animals in the household and support for various attachments including a water bottle, hayrack and toys.

The cage should be cleaned every three days or so. All bedding and newspaper should be dumped, the bottom should be wiped off and fresh bedding should be placed in the cage. If the animal has enough room (about two square feet), then the cage and animal should stay clean. However, if the cavy tends to play with the water bottle, then you may have to clean the cage more often.

Diet

Guinea pigs should be fed a fresh, pelleted food which is plain and contains vitamin C in an appropriate form. The extra "things" that are found in many feeds are not only inappropriate for the cavy, but some are potentially harmful.

Fresh water is essential. The guinea pig's digestive system needs the water to help process food. The water bottle should be emptied and refilled every day—reasonably soft water is recommended. The bottle should also be checked to ensure that algae aren't forming inside or that the nozzle isn't clogged. The bottle should have a steel sipper tube with double ball bearings—this minimizes the amount of dripping that occurs. However, it does nothing to prevent the cavy from playing with the bottle and spilling water all over its cage.

Hay is also an essential food. For young cavies or pregnant/nursing sows, alfalfa hay is acceptable, but for adult guinea pigs, timothy or other grass hays should be used. The high fiber content of hay allows the digestive system to function properly. Alfalfa, with its higher protein and calcium content, is good for the young, but is too rich for the normal adult pig. On the other hand, grass hays have less protein and calcium and provide lots of fiber.

Vegetables should be provided both as treats and to add variety to the diet. The vegetables should be high in vitamin C, low in calcium and high in fiber. In other words, guinea pigs should eat the same kind of vegetables you should be eating. Romaine and other dark green lettuces are good, as well as cilantro, parsley and other herbs. Green and red bell peppers are a wonderful source of vitamin C and other antioxidants, making them a very good treat for the cavy. Carrots and cucumbers are also viable treats. Basically, if it is good food for you, it is good food for them. This means that iceberg lettuce should not be fed to guinea pigs because it has few nutrients.

Fruit should be offered sparingly. Besides the acidity, which can bother a guinea pig's tender lips, fruit usually has a lot of sugar which can cause problems for a guinea pig's digestive system.

Handling

The guinea pig needs to be handled for many tasks. Everything—from removing it from its cage for cleaning to trimming its nails—will require it to be picked up. This handling is rarely an easy process. The cavy is almost as fast in reverse as it is in forward. Since it is a prey animal, it needs to have the ability to move quickly in almost any direction. Add to this information the fact that its skeleton is very light to allow for speed, and you are faced with a fast and fragile animal that needs considerable patience to catch and handle. And no matter how much you love it, there is always a part of its instincts that will react to you as a predator.

Once captured, the guinea pig should always be held with two hands—one below and one above to minimize the possibility of escape and the potential for harm to the animal. The most comfortable position for me to use when moving around with the animal involves pointing the head towards my left elbow, putting the rump on my left hand and covering the shoulders with my right hand. This hold seems to make my animals comfortable as well. The key to handling cavies is that they feel supported and that you have control if the animal should be startled.

When you sit down in a chair or recliner the animal has a nice area to relax and play. This position also allows for some exploring, socializing, petting and other cuddling, as deemed appropriate. Kissing a guinea pig, especially behind the ear on the bald spot, is acceptable behavior. Do not be surprised if you also receive kisses from the guinea pig. The pig's tongue is very small and delicate, but still gives a pleasant sensation (unlike the sandpaper tongue of a cat).

Handling for nail trimming is usually a two-person job. The first person should hold the animal to his or her chest with the animal facing outward (tummy exposed). One hand should be under the rump and the second hand should be just below the forefeet. That person should hold the animal firmly against his or her chest to give the cavy a maximum sense of security. The second person should then do the trimming. I usually trim the front paws first and the back paws second. Pigs often get wiggly after a minute or so, so trimming the big rear nails last decreases the risk of hitting the quick on a squirmy cavy. The quick is a fine blood vessel running inside the nail. Cutting it will cause the cavy to bleed and cry out. You can stop the bleeding by using corn starch or flour and by applying pressure on the toenail.

If you are going to allow a child to handle the animal, you must first take into account his or her ability level. For example, a four-year-old shouldn't take an animal out of the cage, but should have an adult do so. After the animal is removed from the cage, the adult should place the animal on the child's lap (preferably while the child is sitting on the floor with a towel across his or her legs). As a general rule, I suggest that ten is the youngest age when a child should be allowed to handle a guinea pig, and only after he or she receives proper training from an adult. Handling a guinea pig requires some very fine motor skills to avoid injuring the animal.

Behavior

Guinea pigs have a wide range of behaviors that you will want to learn how to recognize—from the familiar "wheek" that indicates their desire for a treat to the madcap "popcorn" that indicates happiness and joy.

Cavies make a wide range of sounds—some are angry or fearful, many are happy or content and some have dual meanings—so you have to be sensitive to the context. A purr while sitting on your lap can be a sign of contentment, unless there is a phone ringing. Over time, you will learn to recognize the sounds and their meanings.

Cavies have an intricate social structure. In the wild they form a herd with one dominant male and his harem. Within that context there is the ranking of the females and the young. This same behavior can be seen in the domestic guinea pig. When you have two females living together, they will determine who is the dominant female. This process can include mounting, as well as some nipping. Female fights are usually not as dangerous as the male fights, but they still need to be carefully monitored in order to avoid injury to the submissive animal. Sometimes there are very dominant females that will harass other animals to the point of death. If you end up with such a female, she should be allowed to live on her own or with a neutered male.

Male fighting can be very dangerous, even deadly. This is not to say that two males can't live together, but it does depend a great deal on their personalities. I once had two unrelated males that lived in harmony and had two brothers that could barely be allowed in the same room together. Male battles often involve a lot of teeth chattering. Since the objective of fighting is to force the other animal to leave the territory, separate cages are often recommended for combative males.

By the way, if you are trying to break up a fight, never insert any part of your body between the combatants. This move is a very good way to learn just how sharp and strong the cavy's teeth are. I now have a lovely one-inch long scar on my right thumb that is my constant reminder of this little rule.

If two cavies are fighting, throw a towel over one or both animals, then pick one of them up in the towel and place him in a separate space.

Grooming

Guinea pigs are generally good about keeping themselves clean, however it is helpful if their cage is cleaned out every three days or so. They often wash themselves as cats or rabbits do. However, there are a few things they could use some help with.

Nails need to be trimmed on a regular basis—monthly would probably be a good schedule, since they tend to develop sharp edges. (Nails can be worn down by including bricks or stones in the environment.)

Brushing can help remove some of the loose hair from a guinea pig's coat. Long-haired breeds like the Peruvian and Silkie should be brushed on a daily basis. Abyssinians (Abys) can be brushed less often and short-haired breeds rarely need brushing. The Teddy and Texel breeds have some unique problems and need special attention when being groomed. We'll talk more about these breeds when we cover grooming in Chapter 6.

A bath is often not needed, although even with the best cleaning habits, cavies will get a bit dirty over time. A bath should be given in warm, shallow water with a gentle shampoo. The cavy should be carefully towel dried and blown dry or placed in a heated area for final drying. Drafts should be avoided since respiratory problems are a major concern for them.

When giving a bath, use a towel or face cloth in the bottom of the bathing container (sink, tub, plastic bowl) so that the cavy has a firm footing. Slippery bottoms will cause it to get anxious. Again, place one hand under the animal's forelegs and use the second hand to wet, shampoo and rinse the animal. When bathing, remember that most guinea pigs do not like water and may try to escape, especially during the rinse cycle. On the other hand, many seem to like the idea of the towel and get very comfortable if they sense a firm footing (like your lap) underneath the towel.

Health

Cavies have a life expectancy of five to seven years, with some living as long as ten and eleven years. Given a proper diet, an attentive owner and a skilled exotics veterinarian, a guinea pig should be able to live a long happy life.

Guinea pigs are prey animals, so they are used to hiding their health problems from the world. After all, a predator is inclined to take out the weakest members of the herd. So the owner must be very alert to the potential problems of their animals. Usually, the first indication of illness is decreased appetite. If you have a cavy that is not eating, get the animal to your vet as soon as possible. The most common health problems include lice, mites and fungal infections. Each of these problems is treatable, if caught early enough. Most of these problems can be spotted during routine grooming sessions.

Pregnancy is also a common problem among cavies that come from pet stores. Few stores keep the sexes separated, so it isn't uncommon to come home with a pregnant sow. Proper diet and a quiet environment will allow her to have a stress free and successful delivery.

The babies are born with fur, open eyes and fully formed teeth and nails. It is not uncommon to see a baby pig eating adult food within a day or two. A little extra protein and calcium in the mother's diet before birth and during the nursing phase will help ensure a healthy family. After the babies are about four weeks old, the two sexes must be separated to prevent additional pregnancies from occurring.

Senior Citizens

Older pigs may need some special care. Weight gain or loss can occur, tooth problems sometimes arise, and boars can have a problem with their anal area. With a little extra care, these problems can be minimized, allowing the cavy to reach a happy and healthy old age.

Older pigs do not process their food as well, so additional care should be taken to ensure that they get ample amounts of vitamin C. You might also consider supplementing their diet with Brewer's Yeast for B vitamins and probiotics.

Naturally, at some point, the guinea pig may either get sick and die or not wake up from a nap. In either case, you will probably feel grief and guilt. This reaction is perfectly normal and appropriate behavior. The guilt comes from playing the "what-if" game—you can't win it, so don't even try. The grief should be recognized for what it is, the loss of a precious pet. Do not listen to anyone who says, "But it was just a guinea pig." Grieving for a pet is normal, whether it's a dog, cat or guinea pig. So allow yourself to feel the sadness.

Chapter Two

Housing

The Cage

Guinea pigs are easy to care for. They require basic care in order to remain content. The cage should have a solid floor, since guinea pigs are "toe walkers" and have bare pads on their feet. When wire floors are used, guinea pigs can get injuries such as broken toes, cut and infected pads and broken legs. A solid floor helps to avoid all of the problems caused by wire flooring.

The cage should have wire sides to allow for adequate air circulation and equipment placement. An aquarium can be used, but the poor ventilation and increased odors makes them less healthful for the cavy. In addition, poor air circulation caused by solid walls with light trapping can cause the inside air to become very warm and potentially deadly to the cavy.

The cage should provide about one-and-a-half to two square feet of floor space for each animal housed in it. So, if you have a single pig, an 18" by 24" cage should be more than adequate (providing three square feet of space). One or two females could live together in such a cage. Once you consider getting more than one animal of the same sex, larger cages become a necessity and, in most cases, they can be made at home with inexpensive materials.

Some cages have a second level that has a wire shelf and ramp. These items should be properly covered in order to prevent any possible foot damage. The material used to cover the ramp and shelf should be easy to clean, like the cage floor. The ramp should have a gentle slope so that the

guinea pig can climb to the second level. Putting a tasty treat on the upper level can encourage initial exploration by the cavies. The shelf adds to the total area, allowing two cavies to live together in a smaller area. Cages higher than two stories need to be carefully evaluated. If they have too much open area, then they can cause falls that might lead to serious injuries.

One way to build a larger cage is with *Neat Idea Cubes* (open frame panels that are used to create "crates") and some cable ties. By tying the sides together, you can create a large rectangular area. By mounting attached cubes on a floor panel with Formica or linoleum on it, you can create cages of various sizes in multiples of one-foot lengths. You can also use wire organizing shelves for the sides and create almost any size cage up to eight feet by eight feet (sixty-four square feet.). This large cage would give you enough room for a big herd.

The floor of a cage should be solid and made of a material that is easy to clean. Most cages have a plastic or metal tray for the floor. Formica and linoleum also work well because they have hard surfaces that are easy to clean. Wood floors are not recommended, because the waste from guinea pigs tends to soak into the wood and create health hazards.

Cavy urine is basic, like baking soda, and often leaves a crystalline residue. Urine can be removed by soaking the residue with vinegar (a mild acid) for about 20 minutes. A putty knife can then be used to scrape off the softened gunk. The entire floor should be wiped down with hydrogen peroxide for complete disinfection. Another very effective cleaner is

Clorox® bleach mixed with water in a 1:20 ratio (the bleach is a very effective disinfectant). After using the cleaner, rinse the floor thoroughly with water. A layer of newspaper and bedding material are put in, making the cage ready for occupancy.

Bedding

Bedding tends to be problematic for many people. The problem lies in the fact that there is much discussion about various materials without a whole lot of proof to back it up. I like to use five to eight sheets of newspaper, covered with an inch or so of kiln-dried pine shavings. I recommend using the black and white sections only because most newspapers have gone to a soy-based black ink. The glossy paper with full color pictures shouldn't be used because it isn't as absorbent and might not be soy-based inks.

Pine is somewhat questionable since it contains aromatic hydrocarbons similar to the ones found in cedar. Kiln-dried pine, which has had many of these aromatic oils removed, is considered a satisfactory bedding. Many breeders use this bedding because it is cheap and doesn't seem to shorten the lifespan of their animals. Any additives, such as chlorophyll should never be used because they can create health problems for the animals. Plain shavings are all that is needed.

Aspen shavings provide a good bedding material for guinea pigs. Although aspen is somewhat more expensive than pine, it does not have the aromatic oils that cause health problems like cedar. While not as absorbent as pine, aspen still provides an adequate bedding material.

Wood stove pellets are also often used, although they tend to be a bit hard on the cavy's feet. These pellets are made of pressed hardwood sawdust, which crumble when moistened. This product provides a very absorbent medium for the cage. If combined with another material such as aspen shavings, you would get the absorbency of the pellets and the soft footing of the shavings.

New alternative materials are also available. *CareFresh* and *Yesterday's News* are two paper type products that offer superior absorbency and good odor control and seem to be hypoallergenic for most cavies and humans. Unfortunately, they are also considerably more expensive than the woods. However, if you have a single animal, these paper materials would be a viable alternative to the wood bedding.

Straw should not be used for bedding. The sharp edges of the stalks can cause injuries to the pads of the guinea pig's feet and can create medical problems. Cavies like to burrow so the straw can also cause eye injuries, which are very difficult to treat. Hay can be used, but it makes a better food source than bedding material.

Corncob is also not a good bedding material. It does not absorb moisture well and creates a breeding ground for bacteria. It is also hazardous if the little ones decide to nibble on it.

Most people agree that cedar, which contains aromatic hydrocarbons, should never be used as bedding. Studies indicate that cedar can cause animal livers to function differently than normal. In other words, when guinea pigs that have been exposed to cedar are given medicine, their livers will not process the medicines properly. Eventually, their livers will deteriorate. So cedar is not an option. In addition, cedar has been shown to contribute to upper respiratory problems and asthma in humans.

Cat litters, especially the clumping varieties, should never be used. Since cavies like to munch on everything in their environment, the clumping litter can create a blockage in their digestive system. Owners should stick to natural products that are more easily broken down by the guinea pig's digestive system.

Food Dish

The food dish should be made out of a heavy material since many pigs love to move their "furniture" around. Light bowls can be tipped over easily. A ceramic dish, preferably with plenty of extra material, would make the best choice. Heavy dishes help keep the pellets in the bowl and remaining fairly clean. If you have a cavy that insists on tipping its dish over, there are plastic dishes that can be clamped to the side of the cage. These dishes can also be positioned a little higher so the animal will not be tempted to sit in the dish and use it as a bathroom.

An alternative food dish is a feeder. Many of these feeders are designed to hang on the inside of the cage. They have little openings or wire mesh on the bottom that allow the pellet dust to fall out. Feeders are easier to fill up and keep clean than bowls and aren't as prone to tippage or bathroom use. Feeders are usually made of sheet metal or plastic. Galvanized metal or aluminum feeders are not recommended because the metal interacts with the ascorbic acid (vitamin C) in the pellets, causing the pellets to deteriorate even faster than usual. Plastic feeders can cause choking or cutting hazards, so owners should keep an eye on their pigs to ensure they aren't chewing or ingesting the plastic. Stainless steel is a great alternative, but is more expensive.

Water Source

Water is essential to the cavy's well-being and health and should be kept clean and fresh at all times. The best way to provide water to cavies is through a clear plastic bottle with a steel sipper tube. The tube should have a double ball bearing. These bottles are less prone to leakage. The water should be refreshed on a daily basis and the bottle should be cleaned on a weekly basis. Clear bottles make it easier to check for water levels and the presence of contamination.

Every time the bottle is cleaned, it should be checked for any algae growth. A great way to clean out algae involves putting about one teaspoon of uncooked rice in with one ounce of water. Shake this mixture vigorously to clean off the scum. Once the scum is removed, the bottle can be rinsed—first rinse with water, then hydrogen peroxide, then water again—and refilled. Once you complete this process, the bottle will be algae free.

An eight-ounce bottle is usually adequate for a single animal. Some guinea pigs drink about an ounce a day, others will empty the bottle twice a day. The key is to watch for leakage—the rubber gasket in the cap should be cleaned off each time the bottle is filled. The bottle's body should be periodically checked for any signs of cracking. Any change in the guinea pig's drinking habits that can't be attributed to bottle problems should be considered a sign that something is wrong. Decreased eating and drinking are often the first signs of a sick animal.

Besides the bottle, you will probably want a bottle guard, which is a sheet metal holder that protects the bottom of the bottle from being nibbled by little pig teeth. The alternative is to mount the bottle on the outside of the cage. This position not only protects the bottle from teeth, but it also makes it easier for you to check the water level. This option is also cheaper because the wire used to hold the bottle on its card in the store can also be used to hold the bottle on the side of the cage. The bottle should be mounted in such a way that the guinea pig has to reach up a bit for it. This action helps the natural flow of the water into the cavy's mouth.

Some people use a water bowl, like the food bowl. The problem is that cavies tend to kick up bedding and other floor stuff when they zoom around the cage. This activity contaminates the water and means that the water bowl needs to be changed frequently.

Hay Rack

Hay is an essential food for the cavy. While many folks simply throw the hay into the cage, you might want to invest in a hay rack, if you use a premium hay. These special wire racks are open on the sides to allow the guinea pig access to the hay. If you place the rack higher than floor level, it prompts the guinea pig to get a little exercise while obtaining its food.

Racked hay stays clean, floor hay gets contaminated. Most pigs can distinguish between hay that can be eaten and hay that shouldn't be eaten. It gets expensive when the hay on the floor has to be replenished and thrown out when the cage is cleaned. If you are buying hay in bales, this may not represent a major expense, but if you are buying the premium hays, it could add up to a significant cost.

Salt Lick

Some people add a salt or mineral lick to the cavy's cage. While few people consider licks to be essential to the cavy's health, they do not usually represent a health risk. The salt lick is often hung from a hook on the hay rack. The brown wheel contains a variety of trace minerals. It isn't clear if salt licks really help the animal stay healthy (although I seriously doubt it), and the licks with added calcium can represent a hazard for a pig prone to bladder stones. The only time a lick might be useful is when the cavy is fed a diet of just hay and vegetables. Quality pellets are usually nutritionally complete in and of themselves (boring, but complete.).

Hideout

Many people like to add a little hideout or house in the cage for the cavy. The problem with this addition is that it encourages the animal to be more skittish—having a place to hide encourages it to hide. You might want to give your guinea pig a hideout for the first week, then remove it during the day and replace it at night. This way, the cavy will have time to adjust to the sights, sounds and smells of its new home.

Some pigs will adjust to life with humans and be very tame even with a house in the cage. If you are lucky enough to get one of these pigs, then you can leave the hideout inside the cage. But most pigs run to their shelter when humans come, no matter how yummy the treat in hand may be. For those pigs, it is probably better to remove the hideout so that they can learn that it is safe to be in the open and roam around.

Cleaning the Habitat

Cleaning the cage and accessories will greatly improve the life of your animal. By keeping the cage and everything in it clean, your animal's grooming will be much easier because it will be able to keep itself cleaner, minimizing the need for you to bathe it, which is usually low on a guinea pig's list of fun things to do. When cleaning the cage, you can do one of several things with the guinea pig. You can let it roam around the room and have some fun catching it after the cleaning. You can put it in another cage or box. Or you can have someone hold it and cuddle it while you clean. Naturally, the last choice is the best for both the animal and the human.

Cage

The cage should have the bedding changed every three days or so. If the cage smells like ammonia, it is past due. A cleaning should include a complete dumping of the bedding material, the newspapers and anything else in the cage. You should wipe down the cage with a damp rag or paper towel. Every week, you should wipe it out with a mild bleach solution, vinegar or hydrogen peroxide. This cleaning will help kill any stray bacteria. When a build-up of calcium carbonate forms where the pig urinates, you will need to soak the area with vinegar for about 20 minutes, then scrape the build up off with a putty knife.

Water bottles

Water bottles should be rinsed out every day and refilled with fresh water. Once a week you should empty the bottle, put in an ounce or so of hydrogen peroxide or a weak bleach solution, and shake it vigorously. This action will kill most of the bacteria that gets into the bottle. If you find that the bottle is developing algae, you can either use a baby bottle brush to clean it out or you can fill the bottle with teaspoon of uncooked rice and water and shake it vigorously when you're finished, dump the mixture and rinse the bottle thoroughly. I have used the rice trick for some time and it does a great job. After you remove the algae, rinse the bottle with hydrogen peroxide or a mild bleach solution, followed by several rinses with water. You want to make sure that all the peroxide or bleach has been removed from the bottle.

Food bowl

The food bowl should be cleaned as needed. If a cavy has been using it as a bathroom, the bowl should be cleaned in hot, mild bleach water in order to get rid of the smell and any bacteria that may be growing. If the pig continues to use it as a toilet, then you should use a smaller bowl or a bowl that hangs on the side of the cage in a high location that makes it difficult for the cavy to sit in. You should also dump and replace the pellets every few days. This dumping gets rid of the fine dust that can accumulate over time.

Toys

Some toys are consumed (like toilet paper or paper towel rolls), while others are not. The non-consumables should be checked to see if they have accumulated any cage gunk and should be cleaned so that they don't become a breeding ground for bacteria. Hanging toys are the best bet since the pigs have to reach in order to play with them. This reaching gives them some exercise, while keeping the toys relatively clean. If you use the toilet paper and paper towel rolls, they should have little or no glue on the outside. Be warned, some pigs love to fling the tubes around, much like an infant who has learned how to throw toys out of the playpen.

Many people put bird toys, the kind with bells and mirrors, in the cage. Others folks provide cat toys, such as the ball with a bell in it. Some pigs love them, some don't. A paper bag with the opening folded back or a small box with doors and windows, also make fun toys for the cavy. There is no limit on the toys that can be used with cavies. Use your imagination, but make sure all toys are practical and safe.

Hideout

Depending on the hideout, you may be able to simply throw it away (cardboard boxes for example) or you may want to wash in hot, mild bleach water. Personally, I don't provide a hideout, so I don't have to clean it. But like everything else in the cage, the hideout should be kept as clean as possible to prevent bacteria from growing.

Chapter Three

Diet

The guinea pig diet is composed of three basic ingredients: pellets, water and hay. Each of these items are essential for normal guinea pig growth and well-being. There are also plenty of treats on the market, however, most of these treats aren't that good for your pet.

Pellets

Simple pellet should be used. The brands with the "extras" are used to entice the human shopper and often are not healthy for the cavy. Many of the mixes include seeds. Guinea pigs will eat the seeds (because they taste good) and ignore the pellets. If you replace the unused pellets with fresh mix, they will continue to eat just the seeds. By doing this, they are getting too much fat and not enough of the nutrients. You should use a plain pellet as the main food and supplement it with other foods as treats (more on that later). The plain pellet should have a protein content of at least 20%—especially true if you are considering breeding.

If possible, use a pellet that has a milled date on the package. Most manufacturers use ascorbic acid for the vitamin C. Unfortunately, ascorbic acid breaks down easily. Sunlight, heat, chlorine and time all cause it to break down. Approximately 90 days after manufacture, most of the ascorbic acid will be gone. There are some companies that produce their pellets with a very stable form of vitamin C. If you can find one of these pellets, use them instead.

Pellets primarily consist of alfalfa which provides good protein and fiber content. However, alfalfa is also high in calcium which may cause problems for cavies prone to bladder stones. Some companies make a timothy-based pellet which is lower in calcium and offers an excellent feed for the adult or "chubby" cavy.

Water

Water is essential for allowing the guinea pig's digestive system to work. The pellets and hay have to be digested, and in the cecum, this requires a nice fluid bed. Water provides that essential fluid.

Water should be kept as fresh as possible. The bottle should be cleaned regularly and fresh water should be given on at least a daily basis. While tap water is generally acceptable, water that is very hard should be filtered for the animals.

In very warm weather, cool water should be provided. The cavy doesn't have a great system for dissipating heat, so cold water can help it keep its systems regulated. One interesting, if unintended, source of cold water can be found by placing a frozen two liter soda bottle in the cage. This frozen bottle provides a nice little air conditioner, and cavies can lick the cold condensation off the bottle. However, this activity should be closely watched. You don't want the animal nipping a hole in the bottle and flooding its cage or eating the plastic label.

Hay

There are two basic hays available—alfalfa and timothy (or grass). The alfalfa is a rich legume hay which has a high protein and calcium content. Alfalfa, therefore, makes an excellent hay for growing youngsters, up to eight months, and pregnant sows. Timothy is a grass hay which has a lower protein and calcium content. This type of hay is ideal for the adult pig.

Hay should be provided for ready nibbling. The cavy is a grazing animal, and therefore will nibble all day long if something appropriate is provided. By offering good quality hay for cavies to eat, you can help them minimize obesity problems that can occur in adult pigs. In addition, this constant grazing keeps the cavy's teeth ground down.

There are many sources for hay. First of all, you can purchase hay at the pet store, but you'll quickly discover that the hay tends to be dry, dusty and over priced. Secondly, especially if you have several animals and have the space for it, you can visit the feed store where hay tends to be highly variant in quality, but very inexpensive. Thirdly, you can go to the local farmers (if you happen to live in an area that has farmers), whose hay is often better than the feed stores because they tend to keep the best for their herd and sell the next best to the feed store. Finally, you can use a specialty hay from companies like *American Pet Diner* or *Oxbow Hay*. These sources are expensive, but the quality tends to be consistently high. If you buy a large amount of hay, say 25 pounds or more, you will find that the per pound cost of Oxbow or APD hay is comparable to the pet store but the quality will be considerably higher.

When feeding these premium hays to cavies, you should use a hay rack in order to minimize waste.

Treats

There are many things that fall under the classification of "treat." Among these items are the boxed treats manufactured by various companies and the treat sticks which can be found in most pet stores. Vegetables and fruit can also be included in this category. Although they are not essential to the animal's well-being, they are nice supplements to the diet.

Treats that are found in the pet store tend to be useless, in my opinion. They are often hard, contain little nutritional value and only serve to separate you from your hard earned money. Some of the treats are actually dangerous to your pet's health. For example, if your cavy insists on eating the honey-coated seed stick instead of its pellets, it will not receive balanced nutrition and will make itself less healthy. Besides which, the seeds are composed mostly of fat which can cause cavies to become obese. (Sort of like humans trying to live on potato chips and soda.)

On the other hand, vegetables and fruits are a great treat, if you serve the right kind and in the right quantities. Dark green vegetables, in fact any dark vegetable, is a good source of nutrients for the guinea pig. My herd loves romaine lettuce, green and red bell peppers, cucumbers and carrots. I also know that many cavies enjoy cilantro, parsley, bok choi and other leafy vegetables. In addition to providing the animal with a variety of foods, so that its life isn't boring, many of these foods are good sources of vitamin C and other vitamins and minerals. These treats are rich in nutrients that are good for the cavy's health, just like they are good for our health.

Care must be taken to ensure that the chosen vegetable is not high in calcium. Some cavies are inclined to form bladder stones, so they need to avoid such vegetables. I also try to avoid the "gassy" veggies or serve them only in small amounts. Some cavies enjoy throw aways, such as the leaves on a head of cauliflower. Cavies are suspicious by nature, so you will probably have to offer a new food for several days before the pig will try it. I like to experiment with new foods by putting a little bit in the animal's mouth so it gets a taste. Sometimes this will interest the cavy and sometimes it will spit the food out and resist it even more.

The following table provides a listing of various fruits and vegetables. This information is taken from the USDA database of foods and is based on a serving of 100 grams (about 3.5 ounces). Since calcium can create problems for some cavies, there is also a column about the calcium content of each food. Naturally, higher vitamin C and lower calcium levels are good for older pigs. However, high levels of both vitamin C and calcium are good for nursing or pregnant sows and young cavies that are still growing. An adult cavy needs about 10 milligrams/kilogram (mg/kg) of body weight per day. Pregnant or nursing sows and babies should have approximately double that amount.

Table 3.1 Vitamin C and Calcium Contents of Vegetables and Fruits
Data from United States Department of Agriculture, 1999.
Each nutrient is based on 100 grams of the vegetable or fruit.

Vegetable/Fruit All Are Fresh and Raw	Vitamin C In Milligrams (mg)	Calcium In Milligrams (mg)
Apple, without skin	4.40	4.40
Apricots	10.00	14.00
Arugula	15.00	160.00
Asparagus	17.69	28.14
Balsam Pear Pod (Also called Bitter Gourd)	13.20	21.00
Banana	9.10	6.00
Basil	18.00	154.00
Beans, Snap	16.30	37.00

Bean Sprouts, Kidney	38.70	17.00
Bean Sprouts, Mung	13.20	13.00
Bean Sprouts, Navy	18.80	15.00
Beet Greens	30.00	119.00
Blackberries	21.00	32.00
Blueberries	13.00	6.00
Borage	35.00	93.00
Broccoli Flowerets	93.20	48.00
Broccoli Stalks	93.20	48.00
Brussels Sprouts	85.00	42.00
Cabbages:		
Domestic	51.00	47.00
Red	57.00	51.00
Chinese/Pak-Choi	45.00	105.00
Savoy	31.00	35.00
Pe-Tsai	27.00	77.00
Carrots	9.30	27.00
Cauliflower	46.40	22.00
Celery	7.00	40.00
Cherimoya	9.00	23.00
Cherries:		
Acerola/West Indian	1677.60	12.00
Pitanga/Surinam	26.30	9.00
Sour	10.00	16.00
Sweet	7.00	15.00
Chicory Greens	24.00	100.00
Collards	35.30	145.00
Corn, Sweet & Yellow	6.80	2.00
Cranberries	13.50	7.00
Cress, Garden	69.00	81.00
Cucumber (with peel)	5.30	14.00
Dandelion Greens	35.00	187.00

Dock	48.00	44.00
Eggplant	1.70	7.00
Elderberries	36.00	38.00
Grapefruit	37.00	15.00
Grapes	4.00	14.00
Grape Leaves	11.10	363.00
Groundcherries	11.00	9.00
(Also known as Poha, Cape Gooseberries)		
Guava	183.50	20.00
Kale	120.00	135.00
Kiwi Fruit	98.00	26.00
Kohlrabi	62.00	24.00
Kumquat	37.40	44.00
Leek	12.00	59.00
Lettuces:		
Butterhead, Boston, Bibb	8.00	32.00
Romaine, Green Leaf	24.00	36.00
Iceberg, New York	3.90	19.00
Loquat	1.00	16.00
Mammy-Apple	14.00	11.00
Mandarin Orange	30.80	14.00
(Also known as Tangerine)		
Mango	27.70	10.00
Melons:		
Cantaloupe	42.20	11.00
Casaba	16.00	5.00
Honeydew	24.80	6.00
Watermelon	9.60	8.00
Mustard Greens	70.00	103.00
Nectarine	5.40	5.00
Okra	21.10	81.00
Onion	6.40	20.00

Onions, Spring Tops & Bulb	18.80	72.00
Orange	53.20	40.00
Papaya	61.80	24.00
Parsley	133.00	138.00
Parsnip	17.00	36.00
Passion Fruit, Purple	30.00	12.00
Peach	6.60	5.00
Peas, Green	40.00	25.00
Pea Pods	60.00	43.00
Pears:		
Asian	3.80	4.00
European	6.60	18.15
Peppers:		
Green Bell Sweet	89.30	9.00
Red Bell Sweet	190.00	9.00
Yellow	183.50	11.00
Persimmon	66.00	27.00
Pineapple	15.40	7.00
Plantain	18.40	3.00
Plum	9.50	4.00
Pomegranate	6.10	3.00
Potato	19.70	7.00
Pumpkin Leaves	11.00	39.00
Quince	15.00	11.00
Raspberries	25.00	22.00
Rhubarb	8.00	86.00
Spinach	28.10	99.00
Spinach, Mustard	130.00	210.00
Squash, Summer	14.80	20.00
Strawberries	56.70	14.00
Sweet Potato	22.70	22.00
Sweet Potato Leaves	11.00	37.00

Swiss Chard	30.00	51.00
Taro Leaves	52.00	107.00
*Tomato, Red	19.10	5.00
Turnip Greens	60.00	190.00
Watercress	43.00	120.00
Witloof	2.80	19.00

Vitamin C values for tomatoes differ depending on variety and season. Table compiled by Louise Czupryna <LMCzupryna@aol.com> 2-23-00

Fruit is not high on my list of treats for guinea pigs. Fruits are usually full of sugars, which cavies don't need. The sugars can get into the cecum, where the fermentation process will work in overdrive, and cause digestive system upsets. As a result, I tend to give small amounts of fruit, if at all. The cavy's mouth has very sensitive skin and too much acid from fruits or tomatoes can cause small sores to form. So go easy on the citrus.

The USDA has a website (http://www.nal.usda.gov/fnic/foodcomp/Data/) that provides nutritional information about many foods. Visit the website and check out the nutrients found in various vegetables and fruits. Since this information is based on human consumption, you won't find guinea pig pellets there, but you might be surprised at what you do find.

Dangerous Plants

There are many plants that are dangerous to your pig's health—usually the plants that represent a health hazard to you or me are also a threat to cavies. As a first rule, a cavy should not eat any plant that comes from a bulb. Avoid any of the nightshade plants, most of the ivy varieties of plants such as Creeping Charlie, hydrangea, yew and other shrubs. Due to their small size, guinea pigs only need a small dose of a poisonous plant to develop a health problem.

Plants with large quantities of oxalates or other such organic compounds should also be avoided. One example is the green areas that form under the skin of a sprouting potato. This growth is dangerous to humans and can be deadly to the little cavy. There are several sites that include information on poisonous plants. Most of them refer to human toxins, which are usually dangerous to the cavy as well. Cornell University has a website at http://www.ansci.cornell.edu/plants/alpharest.html. Another useful resource includes a website designed for rabbits, who share many characteristics with the cavy which can be found at http://home.stlnet.com/~mlhenson/rabbits-398.htm.

The Digestive Process

All of this food and water has to go somewhere. Much of it is used, as in our bodies, for restoration and rebuilding of the body's systems. Since cavies cannot produce vitamin C, they need to have it in their diet. This is why you should feed your cavy guinea pig pellets and not rabbit pellets. Most guinea pig pellets use ascorbic acid for the vitamin C, which tends to break down very easily when exposed to air, light or heat. Therefore, you need to ensure that the pellets you are feeding your cavy are fresh.

Hay benefits guinea pigs because it helps move hair and other indigestible matter out of the stomach and through the digestive system. Near the end of the digestive system is the cecum—a fermentation factory used to break down indigestible fiber, extract essential nutrients and make them available to the cavy's body. Some nutrients are used directly, others are discharged in the form of a cecal pellet—a softer feces that is smaller, darker and consistently smelly. This cecal is reingested by the cavy as it exits the anus. This is known as coprophagy and, while it may sound a bit gross, it is no worse than a cow that regurgitates its cud to chew it after some stomach acid has had a chance to process it a bit. Not eating the cecal pellets can lead to health problems, creating the need to supply additional B vitamins in the diet to assist the animal.

Owners need to closely monitor their cavies when they are taking medication because many antibiotics can impact the balance of the microflora in the system. If too many of the germ positives are killed, the germ negatives get a chance to overrun the cavy's digestive system. This condition often leads to a systemic toxic reaction, often fatal if not treated. **This is why oral penicillin should never be used on a cavy!** Most of the people I have talked to recommend providing some form of probiotic, such as yogurt, to ensure that the cavy's system maintains a proper balance. Another good source of probiotics is *Bene-Bac*™, which contains three germ positive cultures. The probiotic is usually given about an hour or so after the medication.

Cavies get water via the water bottle and vegetables. Obviously water is needed to help the cavy's stomach, intestines and cecum process the food taken in. Water is also essential for clearing out waste matter. Just as urine in humans carries a lot of waste away from the body, it does the same thing in cavies. The difference is that our urine is acidic, while a guinea pig's is basic. That's why cavies can have different problems with their urinary tract. They often have urine that appears white or even orange, however, this coloring is perfectly normal. You should keep your eyes open for the cavy that strains or cries when it urinates. This difficulty could be an early sign of a bladder stone or a urinary tract infection (UTI). We'll discuss these problems in more detail in Chapter Seven.

Chapter Four

Handling the Guinea Pig

The best way to socialize a guinea pig is by handling it. This activity should involve petting and cuddling. Because the cavy is a social animal, it needs companionship to be healthy, and such handling decreases the skittishness of the animal. This handling also benefits humans. In fact, petting an animal has been found to sooth people and reduce blood pressure.

Catching

Catching the guinea pig can turn into a very exciting game. Most of the time humans do not find this activity amusing, and for good reason. The catch can stress both the pig and the human, so it is best to do it as quickly as possible. Of course, the sooner you get the cavy and handle it, the better, and the more you handle it, the more docile it will become. So catch it and cuddle it as often as you can.

The best way to catch the cavy in the cage is to corner it. You should move slowly and prevent it from getting around your hand. Next, you should place one hand behind the cavy, while distracting it with the other hand. Then you should place the distracting hand in front of it. As you move this hand towards the cavy, it will back up. When it reaches the back hand, you should move the front hand quickly to grasp it by the chest and use the back hand to grab its rump.

No matter how you pick up the cavy, the next move is to get it to your chest so that it feels like it has a solid footing again. Once there, you can reposition your arms and hands. My choice for moving from cage to couch is to place the cavy on my left forearm with its head towards my elbow and its rump on my left palm. I then put my right hand over its shoulders to control it. This action offers the cavy a solid footing and lets me move easily, while ensuring that no accidents occur in transit.

Once we reach the safety of the couch, I allow the cavy more freedom. Some pigs will simply settle down for a nice pet and "chubble" happily to you. In fact, you might even get a little purr for your troubles! Other pigs like to explore. Make sure that all surrounding areas are well padded. When a guinea pig tries to get up on my shoulder or onto the back of the couch, I make sure that my shoulder is against the couch and the couch is against the wall so that the cavy cannot fall behind the couch.

Returning

The return can be as difficult as the pick up. Very often cavies try to leap from your hand into the cage from a fair distance (the record for me is about eighteen inches). I try to restrain this action, but it can be very difficult when those little feet are running and scratching up your arm.

Several means can be used to minimize this trauma. First, you can try returning the cavy to the cage rump first. If it can't see the floor, it is less inclined to jump to it. This method is the preferred way, whenever possible. A second way involves covering its face. Most cavies do not like having their faces covered, but the distraction of covering its eyes may give you enough time to get it into the cage before it jumps. Letting it walk down your arm isn't a good option, because most pigs tend to jump and end up banging their faces on the floor. This impact can lead to loose or broken teeth. So special care must be taken to prevent such a crash. I recommend using the same two-handed method for returning as I discussed earlier for removing.

Children

It is great to let children handle a cavy. But, young children and cavies do not always make a good combination. While young children want to hold guinea pigs, they do not have the proper muscle skills or understanding to do so. We all have seen the pictures of a young child carrying a cat by its chest. This looks very cute and isn't particularly dangerous to the cat, but with a cavy, this hold could be fatal. The skeleton of a cavy is much more delicate than that of a cat or kitten. It is designed for speed, not strength and being carried by the chest could lead to cracked ribs, a separated spine or other physical damage.

The easiest way to handle this problem is by locking the cage with a mechanism that takes some skill to open—kind of like the child proof medicine caps—and adult supervision. When a young child (anyone under the age of 10) wants to hold a guinea pig, the adult in the household should take the animal out of the cage, have the child sit down with a towel in his or her lap and place the animal carefully in the lap. Once there, the cavy will probably enjoy the child's petting and cuddling. However, make sure the hugs aren't too strong and do not allow the child to pick up the animal.

The adult in the situation should also handle the return to the cage. In fact, using the towel to remove the animal from the lap may decrease the cavy's stress level until you can get it under adult control again. You should always try to remove the cavy before it decides to use the towel (and the underlying lap) as a bathroom. Many young children will not react well to having the animal urinate on them.

Floor Time

Exercise time on the floor is good for the animal's general health and well-being. Putting guinea pigs on the floor is similar to putting them back in their cage, only it's lower, so you have to manage that "elevator" effect.

It is advisable to make sure that there are no dangers to the guinea pig at low levels. The most common dangers on the floor include carpeting (they try to eat it), plastic in almost any form and electrical wiring. Carpeting is indigestible and can create blockages in the cavy's digestive system. These blockages often lead to either major surgery or death. Cavies have a fondness for plastic trash bags and the plastic covering of wires. I have the severed Nintendo power cord to prove it. So make sure that all forms of soft plastic are safely out of the way. Hard plastics, such as the hard PVC pipes in various shapes and sizes, make excellent tunnels for guinea pigs to play in.

Dangers found on the floor are fairly easy to control. In fact, it's very similar to childproofing a room. You need to remove those hazards that can be removed, and barricade those hazards that cannot. Since a pig can't reach very high, and rarely stands up on its hind legs, wiring can simply be raised up onto high surfaces. Trash bags and other plastic bags can be removed to another room. Other soft plastics can also be elevated or removed. If you watch the pig and see it getting into mischief, just clap your hands and it will be startled and head for cover. Problems can occur if the guinea pig wanders into a hiding place. For example, if the television is on a cart that has a gap underneath, the pig could be hiding in the space and busily chomping on the television's power cord.

One way around all of these problems is to create a contained play area. Some folks use the light plastic toddler wading pools with a three or four foot diameter and 18 inch high walls. The area inside can have various toys including cardboard tubes, stones and large elbow pipes for the entertainment and exercise of the cavy. This option removes all the hazardous problems by confining the animal to a small space. Since this space is larger than the cage, it provides an interesting experience for the cavy. Adding food and water can allow the animal to stay in the play area for an extended period of time. By moving items around or adding new items periodically, the pig is challenged to explore the new environment.

Another option involves using a vinyl tablecloth floor and wire shelving walls to create a play area. The shelving can be fastened together with cable ties or rings. This design provides a fairly large play area that can be broken down for easy storage.

Naturally, capturing the cavy after floor time becomes an adventure. In its new larger space it has much more room to maneuver. If you allow it free run of a room or the house, then the best bet is to try to corner it. I try to herd my guinea pigs into a corner, then lay my body down across the corner and gradually close in on them. This may not look very attractive, but it is the most effective way that I've found. As I catch each animal, I pass it to my wife, who then returns it to its proper cage.

If you are using the pool or other restricted exercise area, the process is a bit simpler, but still more difficult than with a cage. Enlisting the aid of another adult or older child can be very helpful, as long as they don't laugh at you when the pig escapes your grasp by inches!

Nail Trimming

While no one enjoys this job, least of all the cavy, this is an important handling issue. The better the handling, the quicker the trim can be done and the less likely an injury will occur.

I prefer the two-human method. One person holds the animal with the animal's spine against his or her chest. One hand is just below the forelegs and the other hand holds the rump up and secure. The second person does the nail trimming. This process gives that individual the ability to use two hands for each foot, making it easier to control movement and minimize the possibility of cutting the quick. If you cut the front nails first, it goes a bit easier since the pig will start to squirm after a while. To cut down on the number of times you need to trim the front nails, you can add a brick or stone to the cage which can help wear down the nails more quickly. The trimming of the rear feet is often less stressful to the pig.

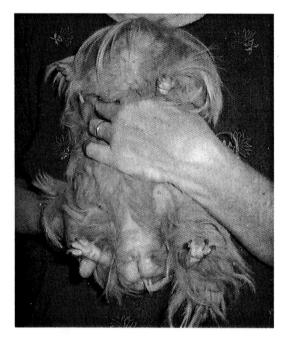

On a clear nail, it is fairly easy to see the pink flesh inside the nail—the quick—and make sure the cut is done below that. However, many cavies have dark nails making it difficult to know where to trim them. I have found that the nail tends to develop a concave area just below the quick. This change is hard to see initially, but with some practice, you should be able to identify this area and make the cut just below it. A second option is to put the clipper on and press it firmly without cutting. If the animal attempts to pull back (more than normal), you are probably over the quick. So you should move down towards the end of the nail and try again. Once you are sure you haven't gotten the quick, cut quickly and firmly. Naturally, some pigs squeak and squirm no matter what part of the nail you are cutting, so adjust your cutting habits accordingly.

For most guinea pig nails, the pocket clippers for human nails work fine. Some pigs have fairly thick nails on the rear feet that will require the guillotine or scissor-type cutters. Whichever cutter you use, always be prepared to stop bleeding from a cut that goes too high. Products like *Quik-Stop* are designed to stop bleeding, but you could also use cornstarch or flour. Some people find that putting pressure on the cut for about a minute also stops the bleeding.

When trimming the nails, you might notice a hard callus off to one side, attached to a pad. You should trim this callus off as close to the pad as possible. There are no blood vessels or nerves in it, but some pigs seem prone to developing these calluses, especially on the front feet. By trimming these growths, you can prevent them from getting torn off or becoming a collection point for dirt or feces. You should also check the feet for any cuts, open wounds or swelling. Early detection of foot problems can prevent them from becoming a serious problem later.

Since you have the animal secure anyway, take a quick look at the belly area. Make sure there aren't any bald areas, scratches, wounds, lumps or other abnormalities that may require a trip to the vet. While the top of a pig is available for inspection on a regular basis, the underside is often neglected.

If you have a boar, use your fingers to gently open his anus and make sure he hasn't collected any debris in there. If you are uncomfortable using a bare hand, obtain a box of vinyl gloves from a drug store and wear one of them. Debris can lead to blockages, which can cause considerable harm. Apply Vaseline or mineral oil using a cotton swab, then remove the debris. You should also check his penis to ensure that it is fully retracted. Some longhaired breeds can get hair wound around the penis, which can be painful and lead to serious infections.

Chapter Five

Behavior

The behavior of the guinea pig is probably one of its most endearing characteristics. It is generally a very affectionate and amiable companion, showing great fondness toward humans. However, sometimes this amiable personality can undergo a terrible transformation.

Much of the guinea pig's behavior originates in the social structure they come from. In the wild, the cavy herd usually consists of a single dominant male with his harem of females and their offspring. When a young male reaches maturity, he may attempt to take over the harem or will be forced out of the group to form his own herd. In the controlled environment of most domesticated cavy set ups, the same young male would have nowhere to go and could be killed by the dominant older male.

The introduction of a new animal to a herd has a similar effect. Not having the "scent" of the existing herd can lead to major problems, so introductions need to be managed with great care. It's important to make the new animal seem like one of the herd before it actually becomes a member.

Familiarity is important in a cavy's world. In the wild, it creates paths that lead to safety and any change in that can spell death. So when you change the bedding in its cage, or rearrange toys or bring a new animal home, you have changed the cavy's environment. Change will cause it some stress, so minimize change and respond to the behavior shifts that may accompany changes.

Sounds

Guinea pigs make a wide variety of sounds. Many of them have double meanings, so it is important to know the context. Many of these sounds provide a warning, either to other guinea pigs (even if there aren't any around) or to the human who is attempting to touch it. Knowing when you are being warned is as important as knowing when you are making the little one happy.

Purr

This sound can have a double meaning. When you are petting the cavy and it purrs, that indicates pleasure. The cavy purr tends to be in short bursts, unlike the cat's continuous one. The purr has the same meaning—considerable enjoyment of whatever petting is going on. The purr that signals danger is usually even shorter and sharper and is often in response to a sudden sound, such as the phone ringing or a door slamming.

Wheek

This sound is apparently reserved for humans. It is often heard in bursts (several wheeks in a row) when the cavy believes that the human is about to provide some vegetable treat. Since many vegetable treats come from plastic bags or from the refrigerator, you will often hear this sound when you bring the groceries home from the store, when you open a bag of potato chips, or when other similar sounds are made. My cavies also make this sound when I'm coming through the living room to the kitchen and on to the family room in the early morning. The sound is usually reserved for humans and is not made towards other cavies.

Rumble

This sound is a very deep purr with a vibrato added. It is most commonly heard when a male is trying to court a female. It is usually accompanied by a slow dance. The male walks towards the female with his rump swaying from side to side. Often this walk is done crab-like from the side. The combination is often referred to as "motorboating" or "rumblestrutting." Either name indicates the same thing, male courtship. This sound is also used by a dominant female to indicate her top position among the other females and by a dominant male towards other males in the cage. My Manda Mae, who was a very dominant pig, would do this to her bonded mate, Spazz. He usually just tried to get out of her way. So if you see one of your guinea pigs doing this to another cavy, the rumbling cavy is usually the dominant one.

Chubble

This is an interesting sound, kind of a combination of muttering and peeping. Often heard during petting, it indicates a degree of contentment, sort of a cavy equivalent of the cat's purr. You'll recognize it is because the cavy will stop making it when you stop petting. The stopping is accompanied by a head turn, which indicates that you should continue your ministrations to the cavy. For some reason, I find this sound to be the most enjoyable one during cuddle time.

Percolating

When a guinea pig is down on the floor and exploring or when a mother has her pups in tow for a bit of adventure, you will hear this gentle popping/percolating sound. I believe it is meant for surrounding cavies to let them know that this particular animal is fine and enjoying a nice walk with no dangers present. The mother will use this sound to give the babies some guidance as to what things are safe for them to visit. Sometimes the sound is more like a cluck than a pop but it has the same intended meaning.

Whistle

The shrill whistle can have two meanings. First, it is a "glad to make your acquaintance" sound, and second, it is used to indicate that the poor cavy is about to be seized by a vicious predator (you!) and all other pigs should hurry to cover. I find that males with a female cagemate tend to make this sound, if they aren't too sure of your intentions. It seems a gallant gesture, but kind of disheartening when they still do it after years of love and affection in your home.

Coo

Difficult to hear, this sound is used by mothers to comfort their babies. It is soft and gentle, so as not to attract any predators, but soothing none the less. When the babies are weaned, the sound usually stops.

Chirp

Some guinea pigs make a chirping sound very much like a bird. No one has been able to determine the cause or purpose of this sound. However, if the chirper has an audience, all members are usually stone still in rapt attention. When the chirping stops, the singer and the audience disperse as if recovering from a trance.

Teeth Chattering

This sound is like a high-pitched woodpecker noise. It clearly indicates that the cavy is agitated and wants you to go away. This sound is often heard between two males and usually accompanies raised hackles, standing tall on the toes (instead of low to the ground, as is normal) and swaying back and forth. This sound represents the first step in male dominance battles that can turn very ugly, very quickly. Do not stick your hand or any other part of your body between two males that are making this sound. I have a lovely one-inch scar on my thumb because I didn't follow this bit of advice. Make a loud noise to distract them and then pick one up as quickly as you can, even if you have to just grab him by the shoulder. Safer still is to throw a towel over them and grab one with the towel. These male battles can get very bloody. Cavies will also chatter at you when you have them cornered during a pick up attempt. Be very respectful of those teeth.

Actions

Just as each sound can have a different meaning, the actions of the animals can also have different meaning in different situation. Most actions accompany sounds and vice versa. The combination should give a clear indication of whether trouble or pleasure is being communicated.

Strut

The strut is used by males to indicate their interest in females. This action is also used in same sex groups where the strutter is trying to establish dominance within the group. I have also seen this behavior exhibited by a female towards the male in her presence, when she is more dominant than him and usually just before she goes into heat.

Hackles Raised

Hackles (the hair on the back of the neck) are raised by two males, and includes standing on tiptoes to make themselves look larger to the other boar. This stance marks the beginning of a fight for the dominant position within the herd—even if there are no immediately available females. The hackles-up-tiptoes-stance is often accompanied by rumblestruting and teeth chattering. At some point, the two males will charge each other and jump into the air, attempting to bite one another.

Mounting

Mounting is normally considered a sexual activity but, as with many other species, it is also used by a dominant animal to display its power over the docile animal. When seen in same sex groups, it indicates that the dominant animal is being very assertive. I have also seen a very dominant female mount a submissive male when she was in heat (he was neutered).

Popcorn

Popcorning behavior is a fun sight—as long as you know what it is. Otherwise, it can scare you. During this action a pig runs around very fast and suddenly leaps straight up in the air, twitching and squeaking. It then lands and takes off again, often in another direction. This activity shows pure joy. Babies start to popcorn when they are about two weeks old or so —they may try it earlier, but they usually fall down instead. Older pigs may also try it, but they are so large that it doesn't have the same effect as when a young pig does it. I've seen this done when cavies have just finished eating a favorite vegetable, when they have gotten some sweet fresh hay, or when they are feeling particularly lively during exercise time.

Nose Touch

When two new pigs meet, especially through the bars of the cage, they touch noses to identify each other. Guinea pigs test the scent of the other animal to see if it belongs to their herd. You can try to fool your cavies by putting some hay or bedding from an existing herd member's cage into the cage of the newcomer for a few days. This hay makes the newcomer smell more like an existing herd member. You can also give both pigs a bath in the same shampoo or dust them with baby powder just before introductions.

Butt Sniffing

New pigs will often sniff each other's butts. I've often seen the dominant pig sniff the submissive pig and give a little push while at it. Often a male will sniff a female to see if she is receptive to mating. If she's not, he's liable to receive more than he bargained for in the form of a well-aimed stream of urine. By the way, some vets have been known to get a good soaking when they inspect a female. So if your vet isn't familiar with cavies, you might want to warn the doctor. Babies will sniff their mother's butt as they wander about the room. This string of pigs is often called a "piggie train." I suspect this activity is to keep the little ones in line behind mom for the initial foray into unknown territory.

Chapter Six

Grooming

Guinea pigs are clean creatures. They try to keep itself well groomed, but because most people do not train it in a litter box (and many people have had considerable success at doing this), they need to have their cages cleaned on a regular basis and be groomed in other ways.

The longhaired breeds need considerable care and attention from their human companion. The Texel, a fairly recent breed, is probably the most difficult to care for. Its long ringlets tend to capture bedding of every variety, requiring frequent grooming sessions. The shorthaired breeds need little care—an occasional brushing, infrequent baths and periodic nail trim—to keep them looking good. (For a complete discussion of guinea pig breeds, please see Appendix A.)

Brushing

The cavy needs to be brushed on a regular basis, just as a dog does. For the shorthaired breeds, brushing can be done with a hand or a soft baby brush. Every time you pet a pig, you are also grooming it. The Abyssinian can be groomed with a baby brush or a small toothbrush. However, because its coat grows in every direction, it is tricky to get it done right.

Peruvians and Silkies (or Shelties in the United Kingdom) are wonderful animals, but their long coats can get tangled or matted. Frequent brushing with a wide toothed brush should be done to keep their lovely coats looking nice. They can also be trimmed during the summer months to help them keep cool. It is not uncommon to see a recently trimmed Peruvian popcorn. While both of these breeds are usually bred for a more

63

docile personality (given their constant grooming needs), they still can get quite upset if you pull out a tangle. Some breeders use a wide-toothed dog comb to work out the tangles. In addition, they might need "spot baths" to clean hair around the rump that may have been stained by urine.

The Teddy (and the Rex in the United Kingdom) can also be groomed with a bare hand. However, brushing is done from rump to head, instead of head to rump as is the case with shorthaired breeds. This brushing style helps their coat to stand up and gives them their characteristic teddy bear look.

The Texel is a hand-groomed pig—you have to hand comb out the mats and tangled bedding. Some folks opt for a shorter coat through hair trims, however, the longer coat is definitely one of the attractions of this breed. Baths can also be very trying—the natural curl and length of their hair can become matted or tangled during washing or drying, so considerable care must be taken with them. These pigs need to be dried under a heat lamp and finger combed only. If you use a brush or comb, the coat will turn frizzy.

A new breed, the Baldwin, has no coat at all, so instead of brushing, these animals need good skin care. Mild skin cream can be used to help them feel better, but it should only be used if the animals are showing signs of skin problems. This breed also has a higher body temperature than most pigs, so these cavies need to be kept warmer and may be more susceptible to colds and other health problems. The obvious advantage of the Baldwin is that it is hypoallergenic, allowing people who may be allergic to cavies to enjoy these loving animals as pets. The Baldwin is not a recognized breed in the ACBA.

Trimming

Some of the longer haired breeds should be trimmed on a regular basis, especially cavies that are not going to be show animals. It is much easier to keep a Peruvian's coat detangled, if it is short. The best way to trim hair is with a pair of blunt-nosed scissors—moustache scissors are moderately blunt, but you may want to use bandage scissors until you get good at it. You should only take off a little at a time. You can always trim more but you cannot put it back. Also, you should be very careful around the animal's face. There are several whiskers around the head that apparently are used for sensing proximity to things. If you trim one of these by accident, it could cause the pig to have some navigating problems. Naturally, be very careful around the genital area, which tends to be a sensitive area for all animals.

If you are very talented and have a particularly docile pig, you can try doing some styling. However, for most cavies, just getting the tangles out will be sufficient. If you are planning to show your pig, contact a breeder who raises that particular breed and have him or her show you how to do wrapping. This process is interesting, but it should not be tried without careful instruction. Wrapping is similar to using rollers in a woman's hair. It uses a small piece of cloth and rubber bands or small hair clamps to get the hair up off the floor and minimizes the need for bathing and combing. Done properly, wrapping can give a very attractive wave to a Peruvian's or Silkie's coat when taken down.

Nail Trimming

As mentioned earlier, nail trimming is usually a two-person job. If a second person isn't available, then the "burrito" method is recommended. First, you should take a towel and drape it over the pig, wrapping the animal snuggly, so that it has a hard time squirming. Next, turn the pig over and take a single foot out so that it can be trimmed easily. As you trim each foot, be careful not to cut the quick. If you should cut the quick, have some flour, cornstarch or *Quik-Stop* available to stop the bleeding. If the cavy does bleed, you can press some of the powder on the wound and apply pressure until the bleeding stops. This bleeding looks a lot worst than it actually is, but it is still traumatic to both the cavy and you.

After trimming each foot, try to get the trimmed foot wrapped and take out a new foot to trim. Naturally, the pig will be fighting you all the way. Often, I've had the pig get both front feet out and while trying to trim a nail, I've gotten nipped or scratched for my troubles. The rear feet do not seem to upset the animal as much, probably because it can't see the rear feet as easily as the front ones.

If you are fairly comfortable with your handling skills, you can try doing the job without the towel. I have had good success with putting the cavy's rump on my left elbow, using my left hand to hold the chest of the pig against my chest and doing the trimming with the clippers in my right hand.

When you are done with the trimming, give the animal some cuddles and a treat. Try to make the total experience as pleasant as possible. That way, maybe it won't be so upset the next time.

Baths

Cavies don't need to be bathed frequently. However, they do tend to get a bit oily after a while, so a bath may be in order. Bathing can be a very trying event for the pig, so get it done as quickly and with as little trauma as possible. In fact, try to make it a fun event—after the bath is a great time for some great cuddling and treat giving.

A bath should be fairly warm. The cavy's body temperature is around 101°F to 103°F compared to our 98.6°F, so bath water should be a bit warmer than you would use for a human infant. You should put an inch or two of water in the tub or sink and place a towel or face cloth on the bottom of the bathing area in order to create a non-slip surface for the cavy's feet. Using your hand or a cup, soak the animal's body with warm water, then apply shampoo, working up a good lather over the entire body including the shoulders and hips. Make sure you lift up the cavy to get a good lather on the belly. Try to avoid getting any soap in the pig's eyes or ears. (Some folks will put eye drops or glycerin in their eyes to protect them.) Baby shampoo can be used effectively. Since the cavy's skin is very sensitive, harsh shampoos should be avoided because they dry out the skin and cause other problems.

The cavy should be rinsed off with clean water. Make sure that all the soap is out of the fur, then towel dry with a large towel, working to get the maximum amount of water out of the fur. At this point, many people do one of two things—either they use a blow dryer or a heat lamp to dry the animal. Personally I like to use the blow dryer and try to hold the pig on a dry towel during the drying process. If the coat is somewhat long then it's a good idea to brush it out and make sure that no tangles form.

Males can have a special problem. They have a scent gland just below the area where the spine takes a sharp turn down, just above the anus. This gland produces a heavy wax and is quite smelly. This material can be removed in many ways. First of all, the larger clumps can be removed by hand, but be careful not to pull too much hair in the process. Secondly, you can use a degreaser which can be found in most automotive stores to remove the excess grease before the regular bath. Once the scent gland is degreased, then the boar can be given a regular bath. The bath removes any residual degreaser and helps him feel more comfortable. Some people use *Dawn* dishwashing soap for the scent gland, because it cuts grease well and is fairly mild on the skin. The *Dawn* cleaning should be followed by a normal bath to get all of the residue out of the cavy's coat.

Things to Do While Grooming a Pig

Along with whatever grooming activity you are doing, you should use this opportunity to do some other inspections. While trimming the nails, check the footpads to make sure there are no wounds, swelling or cracking. Bumblefoot (discussed later) is a major problem for many animals, and early detection is very important.

While grooming you should also look at the animal's eyes to make sure they are still bright and clear. Check for any cloudiness which can indicate an infection or injury. Look for any inflammation of the eyelid because this can also indicate an infection or that something may be caught in the eye. Check to ensure the nose doesn't have any discharge—a clear discharge can be the first sign of an allergy and a discolored discharge can be the first sign of an upper respiratory infection (URI).

Also check the incisors to make sure they meet properly and that none have been broken. The incisors should show even wear and meet smoothly. If you look straight at the mouth, the tips of the top and bottom teeth should have a horizontal edge, any angle would indicate that the animal is chewing abnormally and needs to have its premolars and molars checked by a veterinarian.

While giving a bath, complete a whole body inspection. Check for any bumps, scabs, bald areas, etc. All of these conditions are hints that the pig may need medical attention. You can also use bath time to clean out any wax build up in the ears. Sometimes wax is the first sign of ear mites. If a normally clean-eared pig has heavy wax, it may be time for a vet visit to check for ear mites. Bumps and scabs indicate possible wound sites. Bumps can be the first sign of a cyst or abscess. If you find a bump, keep an eye on it for any changes. If it changes size or shape, get your animal to your vet for an immediate evaluation. If the bump doesn't change size or shape or cause any pain when touched, have your vet check it at the pig's next appointment.

Medical issues will be covered in greater detail in the next chapter, but it's important to remember that a cavy is very good at hiding symptoms when in trouble. It has to hide its weakness to minimize the possibility of a predator picking it out for culling. Yes, it has been several hundred years since cavies were prey animals, but that kind of "hard coding" doesn't go away that quickly. So you should take every opportunity to check your animal for possible health problems. Don't get paranoid about it, but do be conscious of any changes in your animal's eating, drinking or activity levels. Any change could be a sign of a problem. If your instinct says something is wrong, trust it, especially if your cavy is an animal you have spent a lot of time with. No one knows your cavy's normal condition better than you do.

Chapter Seven

Health

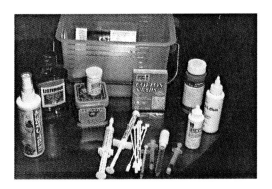

The cavy is supposed to have a life expectancy of five to seven years. There is a fairly high death rate for young animals due to children's mishandling, poor adult supervision, or poor environmental factors, such as using cedar for bedding. Hopefully, the suggestions I have made throughout this book will help your animal survive to the higher end of the age range. With a knowledgeable owner and a competent exotics vet, the chances of your cavy living to a ripe old age are significantly improved.

First of all, you have to take into account that guinea pigs are prey animals. They are very good at hiding ailments or injuries. By the time you see the cavy sitting in a corner with glazed and slitted eyes and a ruffed coat, it is almost too late. A high degree of vigilance on the part of the animal's human companion is essential to the cavy's survival. Secondly, a good vet needs to be found, and this task is not always easy. The study of cavies is not seen as a high priority at most vet schools. They believe that the cavy is not a good survivor, when in fact, low cavy survival rates have more to do with poor recognition on the part of the owner, little knowledge of cavy physiology or diseases and lack of aggressive treatment by the vet. We will talk more about finding a vet later in this chapter.

In one instance, I spent nearly $1000 on a single animal. I consider the cost to be well worth the effort. I had to be knowledgeable about what was happening with the animal and had vets that were willing to fight with me for her survival. Because I was willing to fight for my little Manda Mae, and my vets were willing to work with me to save her, we gave her another year and a half of quality life with plenty of love and affection. If the vet isn't willing to fight, then you are at a considerable disadvantage, and having a seriously ill animal is not the time to find this fact out. I lost one cavy because the vet I went to was not aggressive in treating a large stone. I will not let this happen to me again.

General Health Issues

The cavy needs a healthful environment to thrive in and live happily. The food, housing and exercise that we discussed earlier help in this regard. However, you also have to take into account some other things. Cavies are very sensitive to heat and drafts, so their cages should be set up where they are not exposed to direct sunlight and drafts. These precautions help prevent heat stroke and respiratory problems. The cage needs to be cleaned out regularly to minimize the accumulation of waste and the build-up of ammonia. Keeping the vegetables fresh and varied keeps cavies mentally stimulated. Any uneaten vegetables should be removed before they have a chance to become spoiled in the cage. Exercise prevents the cavy from becoming fat or getting out of shape. You should also provide toys for mental stimulation including cardboard tubes, lengths of hard plastic pipe and paper bags. All of these materials provide cavies with objects to explore and chew on. Cat and bird toys can also be used successfully. During floor time many cavies enjoy playing with cat balls that have bells inside. Guinea pigs also have been known to use hanging bell toys as a means of calling their human when they want a treat. Cardboard tubes stuffed with hay, also provide entertainment for the cavy as well as a healthy food snack.

It is a good idea to interact with your animal on a daily basis. Picking up your cavy for a little petting and cuddling session helps the animal to feel secure in your presence and allows you to enjoy your little one. In addition, you can use this time for a quick survey of its state of health. Look at the coat and eyes, check that they are shiny and clear of any problems. The coat should have good coloring and condition—this is your first line of defense against disease. A good coat and clear eyes generally indicate a healthy animal. One of the first signs of stress in a cavy is excessive shedding. This shedding may be what triggers you to do a more thorough examination of the animal.

Check the nails and teeth on a regular basis and watch for any broken teeth or nails. Such breakage can be an early sign of scurvy or other medical problems. Scurvy symptoms include a flat coat, listlessness and soft or brittle bones. The best treatment for this disease is a course of large quantities of vitamin C and an increase in the daily intake of vitamin C.

Check the pads of the feet because a small cut can lead to major infections later. Some cavies tend to develop horny growths on the side of their footpads. These growths should be trimmed back to minimize the possibility of having them get caught or torn off.

Checking the cavy's waste output is also critical. Firm and well-formed feces indicate that the digestive system is working properly. Remember, a guinea pig has two kinds of feces—the firm waste variety and the reingested cecals. The latter provides the cavy with essential vitamins and proteins after the fiber has been digested in the cecum. The cecum can be compared to the latter stomachs in a cow. Just as a cow must regurgitate its cud after partial digestion, so the cavy must reingest the cecal droppings. If you are finding cecals around the cage, then the cavy is getting a too-rich diet. You should cut back on the alfalfa and pellets and increase the grass hay intake. If the cavy shows signs of diarrhea, you should cut out all vegetables until the feces are firm again. Any sustained diarrhea is a serious health danger, and rehydration and electrolyte replacement will be a necessary part of the recovery process. If a cavy is suffering from diarrhea for more than two days, a trip to the vet is essential.

Common Problems

Most of the following problems can be dealt with by an alert and conscientious owner. However, it is always a good idea to check with your veterinarian about what is the problem and correct treatment. It is always a good idea to have a good vet that you trust that can help you take proper care of your animals. Whenever you are in doubt, take the animal to the vet. If your gut tells you something isn't just right, go to your vet. Better to have your vet think you are a "nervous Nellie" than to lose your pet from delaying treatment.

Lice

One of the most common problems for cavies is lice. The lice cavies get are "species specific," so they will not transfer from the cavy to the humans in the household. Lice do need to be treated because they will cause undue stress and discomfort to the cavy. The first indication of possible lice problems will be a grumpy, itchy cavy. The louse looks like a small grain of rice that moves. They are white, grey or light brown in color. Lice do not like to be exposed to light, so you can only find them by brushing the hair back the wrong way around the rump or neck and watching for the "moving rice." (The rump and neck are the easiest places to check.)

Treatment for a lice infected cavy usually involves a bath in a gentle flea and tick shampoo, a spray with an anti-tick chemical in it (such as pyrethrins) or an injectable treatment such as ivermectin. I have also used the bird flea and tick spray with considerable success. I find that spraying the coat (making sure that no spray gets into the cavy's eyes or nose) and working the spray down to skin level works very well. I make sure that the folds at the hip and shoulder are sprayed. You can also apply spray with a small toothbrush so that the face can be treated without danger of getting the chemicals in the animal's eyes or mouth. After spraying, I wipe off the excess and let the spray dry on the animal. Usually one spraying is sufficient to kill all the lice and larvae as they hatch.

Remember to spray or otherwise clean the cage, cage wiring, food bowl, water bottles, toys and other things in the cage as well. All wood and cardboard should be disposed of or treated. I use the spray on the cage, cage wires and cage table. Clean all food bowls, bottles and chewable items with a diluted bleach solution and then rinse thoroughly with water.

Lice are generally transmitted from an infected pig to a healthy pig. This fact is one reason for quarantining a new animal. You should always check for any signs of lice or other problems before introducing a new pig to your existing herd.

Mites

Mites are the second most common problem for cavies. It seems that mites live in a delicate balance on every cavy and are only able to surge up and create a problem when the cavy's health is compromised in some other way (such as pregnancy, upper respiratory infection or urinary tract infection). The easiest and best treatment for mites is to have the vet give the animal a series of ivermectin injections. Dr. Richardson's excellent book *The Diseases of the Domestic Guinea Pig* provides information about the necessary dosing levels. (See the Bibliography for more information about this book.)

Mites cannot be seen. However, when mites are present, the cavy becomes irritable, scratching more than usual and showing signs of dull hair and coat loss with irritated skin underneath. A skin scraping rarely shows the presence of mites. However, since ivermectin has no major side effects if given at the proper dose, and if no other problem seems plausible, you should go ahead and have your vet treat for mites if you suspect they are present.

Some people believe that lice and mites can be transferred via hay or bedding materials. I doubt this for several reasons. First, most species of mites and all species of lice are host-specific, so it would only be possible for them to get into the hay or bedding from guinea pigs that previously lived in the hay or bedding before packaging. Second, hay is dried for a long period and then baled or processed before sending to users. This process would require the mites or lice to be in a dormant state for some time. Bedding, especially pine, is heat treated (kiln dried) and *CareFresh* and other such materials are heavily processed, many of which probably involve either high temperatures or harsh chemicals. All of these situations suggest to me that the mites and lice would have a very difficult time surviving in the hay or bedding materials.

Fungal Infections

One thing that can be mistaken for mites is a fungus. Ringworm is not uncommon in cavies, especially if they are offered opportunities to be outside. Unfortunately, ringworm is transmittable to humans, so care must be taken in handling infected cavies. Some fungi will glow under a "Woods Lamp," so have the vet check for fungi first. A culture can also be taken to see if it will grow a fungus. This culture can take some time to grow, so if a fungus is found, you should follow normal fungal treatment procedures according to your vet's advice and supervision. However, be very careful not to get yourself infected.

Scurvy

Also known as vitamin C deficiency, scurvy is caused by insufficient vitamin C in the cavy's diet. While guinea pig pellets are supplemented with vitamin C, they can lose potency fairly quickly, especially in hot, humid weather. The best way to prevent this problem is to supplement the animal's diet with high vitamin C foods. Some of the best foods include red and green bell peppers, kale, leaf lettuces, etc. Some of the worst foods include fresh fruits and iceberg lettuce (refer to the table in Chapter Three). The signs of deficiency include stiffness, walking difficulties, general discomfort and paralysis. Another sign of vitamin C deficiency is a lackluster coat or skin. This disease can also be responsible for weakening the ligaments that hold teeth in bone, thus causing teeth to rotate toward the tongue creating a whole new set of problems.

To relieve the problem, you need to provide high doses of vitamin C to the animal. Several methods are available—you can add drops to the cavy's water, but the chlorine destroys the vitamin C fairly quickly; you can provide more of the high vitamin C veggies, but this can cause diarrhea; or you can feed a cavy a chewable tablet. One trick that works for me involves crushing the tablet and spreading it on cucumber slices. The cavies seem to enjoy this treat. Watch out for the tablets with too much sugar, because the cavy's system doesn't process sugars very well.

Pregnancy

This condition is an all too common occurrence, usually caused by ignorant

pet shop employees, lack of care on the part of the wholesaler or "accidents" in the home. Please refer to Appendix B for my opinion on breeding. The cavy sow goes into heat every 16-18 days. Gestation lasts from 65-70 days, however some reports state that gestation can last as long as 72 days. The pups usually can be felt fairly early. They feel like small nuts and their skeletons are easily discernable about six weeks into the pregnancy. Birth comes about three weeks after the pups begin to move. When the sow is about to give birth, her pelvic bone separates, causing her body to flatten. She often looks like a dinner plate with a face. Do not be fooled, she can still move pretty quickly if need be. When the gap between the pelvic sections is a good finger's width apart (around 2 cm—almost an inch), birth should occur within the next three days. The best way to feel this gap is by picking her up —very gently— and running your long finger down her centerline with the other fingers spread to support the babies. Just in front of the vaginal opening, you can feel the points of the pelvic bones. They separate to a centimeter for a week or so and then finally move out to the full two centimeters.

Delivery takes very little time. A litter of four can be delivered in as little as a half an hour. The mother will break the sac over the pup's mouth and nose so it can breathe, deliver the next pup and break its sac, and so on until all the babies are born. As she has opportunity, she will remove more of the sac by licking the babies clean. After the births, she will discharge the placentas—one for each baby. She may eat part of or all of the placentas. This act does two things—it stimulates her to start lactating and it removes evidence of the birth. There may be some blood around the vaginal opening. The mother will usually clean herself up but if there are still signs of blood after a day you should give her a spot bath.

Sometimes you will see her batting one of the babies around. This rough handling is to stimulate the pup to breathe on its own. If she gets too busy to open the sac of the next baby born, you can do this for her by pinching the sac with your fingernails directly in front of the mouth and pulling it back off the head. Once the baby starts breathing and moving, leave it be so the mother can finish the cleaning and birthing process.

Babies are born with their eyes open, a full coat of fur and teeth and nails ready to use. They often wobble about when first born, but are fairly stable on their feet after an hour or two. Babies can be picked up when they are dry, about an hour after birth. The mother will not reject them or attempt to kill them if you handle them at this time. Baby cavies are the most adorable critters around—looking like caricatures of adult cavies with oversized ears and feet.

The best thing you can do during and after birth is ensure that the mother has the best possible chance of doing a good job on her own. Yes, she is young (the accidentals usually are) and isn't totally grown up herself. But she will do fine if you give her good care leading up to the birthing day and remain very alert that final day (I have been faked out twice). She needs to have good quality pellets, good hay, fresh water and vegetables. You want to provide her with twice the normal amount of vitamin C and extra calcium. Feeding her spinach and kale can do this. Both have high levels of vitamin C and calcium. These extra supplements should be continued until she is finished nursing the babies.

You may also want to provide her with sweetened water. Molasses or *Karo* Syrup can be used—about a teaspoon of the sweetener to eight ounces of water. This mixture should be provided in a bowl or bottle along with the normal water. The extra sugar is thought to help prevent pregnancy toxemia, a condition that is usually fatal. You can also provide her with some alfalfa hay, if you feel that she needs extra calcium. However, timothy hay and normal pellets should be fine. Be careful not to provide too much calcium, because it can lead to bladder sludge or bladder stones.

Once the babies are born, they will nurse for three to four weeks. Around the second day, they will start eating other foods, and by the end of the first week, they will eat pellets, drink from the water bottle and eat vegetables without much difficulty. They should have a good amount of vitamin C and calcium in their diets, too. At about four weeks, they should be separated by sex. While it is a little unusual for a boar to be fertile at that young age, it can happen. You do not want a young boar to impregnate either his mother or sister.

If you have a male and female guinea pig, you should not keep the male with the female at all. She comes into heat an hour or so after delivery.

The last thing you need is a sow trying to nurse one litter and carrying a second. When the pups are young, they can visit the male. He will make an excellent babysitter, while you give the mother a break from the babies. At four weeks, when you separate the sexes, you can put the sons in with their father, and the daughters can stay with their mother

Bladder Stones

Bladder stones are a fairly common and poorly understood problem with guinea pigs. The current thinking is that a low water intake contributes to stone formation by allowing the calcium carbonate to precipitate out. There is also the possibility of a genetic component to this problem. The stones cause irritation of the bladder walls, leading to a urinary tract infection (UTI). The infection can be treated, but until the stone is removed and the low water intake problem is solved, it can become a recurring problem. Part of the solution involves providing a good balance of nutrients, while minimizing dietary calcium. You should feed low-calcium vegetables and probably shift to timothy-based pellets. Increasing the water intake may be accomplished by flavoring the water with a sweet juice, but then you risk having the cavy become overweight.

Upper Respiratory Infections

Upper respiratory infections (URIs) are a very common problem for cavies. It is believed that they do not share most of the viruses and bacteria commonly associated with human URI, but it is better to play it safe. When you have the flu or a cold, minimize the handling of your animal and make sure that you wash your hands before and after handling your cavy to reduce the possibility of disease transmission.

Sometimes an allergy is mistaken for a URI. Allergies usually involve clear discharges from the eyes or nose or both. URIs will usually have a discolored (yellow or green) discharge from the nose and sometimes a crusty build up around the eyes.

URIs should never be taken lightly. As soon as you see the runny nose and watery eyes, go to the vet and have the animal checked out and put on an antibiotic, if needed. Many animals are lost when the owner delays seeking medical care. Pneumonia is common and often fatal if not treated quickly. Sulfa-based antibiotics have a very good success rate with pneumonia. One of the primary indicators of pneumonia is a click in the breathing. You can listen to a cavy's breathing by holding it to your ear. Good breathing has a faint sound to it, distressed breathing sounds labored, and pneumonia has a click present.

Malocclusion

Malocclusion is the situation where a cavy's teeth do not wear evenly and create dental problems. Often the problem occurs when some other disease causes the cavy to go off its feed. The teeth are not doing thier work and can overgrow, causing the cavy to chew improperly.

Sometimes a mouth sore or abscess will cause the cavy to favor one side or the other when chewing. This situation becomes apparent when the incisors show an angled edge instead of the usual horizontal alignment.

In order to find the cause of malocclusion you need to have the affected animal evaluated by your vet. Once a cause is identified, you can figure out how to handle it. Filing the teeth can usually take care of most problems, but make sure the filing doesn't create more problems by causing sores in the mouth.

The Cambridge Cavy Trust in the United Kingdom has developed a set of tools for trimming teeth without having to use anesthesia on the cavy. Unfortunately, the tools are not readily available in this country. Work with your vet to figure out how best to handle this problem and be prepared to face this ongoing task.

Impaction

Impaction is strictly a male problem (at least I've never heard of a female having it). And to complicate things, there are two different health problems associated with this condition.

The first kind of impaction is relatively simple to deal with. When a male is marking for courtship purposes, he opens his anus and rubs a very smelly, sticky substance on the floor. You can see this scent gland when he is doing it because it looks like a white ring around his anus. When there is bedding and other materials in the way, they can be picked up and become lodged in the anus. This debris can affect his normal defecation. So when you are checking your pigs, look at the inside of the male's anus and make sure there isn't anything stuck inside. Pay special attention to the males that love to mark their territory. If your boar isn't inclined to mark and attract females, he probably will not have this problem. The younger boars seem to mark more often, so they are more prone to this form of impaction. To clean an impacted anus, gently pick away the material or apply some mineral oil or Vaseline to soften the sticky substance and remove the debris. Make sure you don't tear the skin, because that can lead to an infection.

The second form of impaction is more worrisome. Some unneutered older boars (over two-and-a-half-years-old) develop weak muscles in their anus. Some literature suggests that geriatric sows may also have this problem. Their weak muscles allow the cecals (the soft, smelly ones) to collect in a little sac there, often blocking the anus and causing all feces to get caught in a big mass. If this mass isn't cleaned out, it can lead to severe health problems and even death. The only solution is to express the mass, by lubricating the anus with something like Vaseline or mineral oil, then gently pressing the mass out. When the mass has been removed, you should take a Q-tip and smear the inside of the anus with the lubricant. More than likely the problem will persist, and you will find yourself cleaning him out every few days. I once had a rescued boar that required this attention twice a day. By cleaning the blockage out, you are preventing the entire digestive system from backing up. Some things that can help minimize this problem include encouraging more hay eating, decreasing pellet intake (since high protein diets contribute to more cecal production), decreasing or eliminating carrots and other high starch foods, and as a last resort, having the cavy neutered.

An impacted cavy is missing the essential nutrients that are contained in the cecals. If another boar is available who is overproducing cecals, then you can feed some of the extra cecals to the one with the problem. This cecal intake will help the impacted animal maintain a healthy system. You can also provide a probiotic to help the cecum work more properly and use Brewer's Yeast to replace the B vitamins that are lost in the cecals.

Enteritis

During enteritis, the digestive system seems to shut down and produce a serious gas build-up. Signs of this condition include a distended abdomen, discomfort, lack of appetite, lack of bowel movement and a lowered body temperature. This condition is life threatening. You should first try to get some simethicone into the animal in order to break up the gas and then call the vet. Try to get the animal warmed up by putting it on a towel over a heating pad at a low setting or inside your shirt. Give the animal room to move off the pad, you do not want to risk burning it. You can also put the guinea pig in a cage with a heat lamp. If nothing is available, put it inside your shirt. Try to force some *Pedialyte* into it with an eyedropper. Treatment is necessary as quickly as possible to improve the chances of survival. Treatment will probably involve force-feeding and rehydration. Great care should be taken to ensure the body temperature is kept up.

Ovarian Cysts

Cysts can occur anywhere on the body and are usually benign. However, ovarian cysts can be deadly. They can appear at almost any age in a sow's life. Naturally, they can only occur in a sow that hasn't been spayed.

One of the most common symptoms is bilateral loss of hair on the abdomen just in front of the rear legs. While each side's loss may be a different size or shape, for some reason it is bilateral. The skin will not be irritated, but will be smooth and soft, thus distinguishing it from a mite problem. You can ask for an ultrasound, which is expensive and not always conclusive, or simply have the animal spayed. If the cysts are not removed, they can burst, leading to an infection and ultimately death.

Pea Eye

Pea eye is a condition where some eyelid tissue pushes out into the eye area. It looks awful but is totally harmless. It does need to be watched to ensure that bedding or other debris doesn't get caught there and lead to an eye injury or infection.

Finding a Vet

Finding a vet for your guinea pig is a great adventure that can often be frustrating. Apparently, the study of guinea pigs and all other exotic pets is a very small part of the vet's training and practice, so finding a vet who knows and understands guinea pigs is very difficult.

You should start by calling several vets in your area. Ask them if they know of any vets who either specialize in guinea pigs or at least have a good working knowledge of them. If several vets mention the same person, then you are well on your way. Set up an appointment with the vet for a well animal visit and general discussion. Make it clear to the vet that you are interviewing for the position of your cavy's doctor.

When you take your animal to the vet, ask all kinds of questions. See how knowledgeable the vet is about the cavy. Ask such questions as: Do you have pets of your own? Have you ever had a cavy? How many cavies do you see on a regular basis? How many "exotics" do you see on a regular basis? Do you have cavy surgical experience? If so, what is it? Ask questions that you already know the answers to and see if the vet knows the answers as well. Naturally, a caring and friendly vet with a kind and compassionate staff gets extra points. If the vet is willing to take your third degree, and also seems capable of handling your pet with competence, then you may have found your vet. You also need to make it clear to the doctor what your level of commitment is to your animal. If you are willing to fight for your animal's health, the doctor should be too. I quit seeing a doctor because he was not aggressive enough in treating a sow with ovarian cysts.

Once you have found the vet, try to establish a rapport with the doctor. If you join on-line groups that discuss animal health issues, you can give your doctor information that you obtain. Just make sure that the information is reliable. I had a boar with impaction. He developed bumblefoot—a very serious foot infection which usually takes a lot of work to get under control—so I checked with several on-line groups about treatment. Several people sent back, "My piggie had that and my vet used 'X' and it helped a lot to clear up the problem." I took the various choices with me to my next vet visit, the doctor reviewed the information and we agreed on a course of action. So my vet is willing to learn from other's experiences. Willingness to learn is always a plus.

If you find a good vet, hang on to him or her. Let others know that this vet seems to be very knowledgeable about guinea pigs and works with the client to ensure the cavy has a long and healthy life. That way, your vet gets to be even more experienced.

Try to locate a good vet when your animal is healthy, because looking for a vet during a crisis is always difficult. You will often lose the animal before you find the vet and that can be devastating.

Giving Medications

Probably one of the most difficult tasks to do with a cavy is give it medication. This process usually involves turning the cavy over and forcing something into its mouth–both actions are not welcome by the animal. Peter

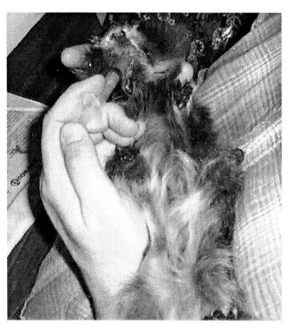

Gurney encourages owners to use the "piggie burrito," which requires wrapping the pig snuggly in a towel. While this often works, I find that cavies can get their front feet out fairly easily. What I prefer to do is to hold the pig with its rump towards my left elbow and trapped next to my body. I use my left forearm to restrain the body and my right hand to restrain the head. I then administer the medicine to the side of the mouth with my left hand. Naturally, this system works well for me because I'm left handed. It should work equally well for a right-hander working in the opposite direction. This scheme also allows me time to do a quick visual inspection of the underside of the pig.

When I give pill-form medicines, I simply crush them in a teaspoon with 0.2cc of water, making the mixture into a thick paste. I then add another 0.5cc of water and mix this solution with the end of the syringe. This thin liquid is easily sucked up into the 1cc syringe that I use to dispense the medicine. I give the medicine in small amounts, encouraging the cavy to swallow it by placing the tip of the syringe against the side of its tongue. After all the medicine is given, I provide about 0.5cc of water to clear out the residual medicine in the syringe and help the cavy get rid of the bad taste in its mouth. I also give the guinea pig a small piece of a treat food, usually green pepper or parsley, which also helps clear out the medicine taste.

Sometimes, you will get an animal that is willing to take the medicine whole or in pieces. In that case, I will turn it over and push the pill back until I can feel the first premolar. When the pill gets past these teeth, the cavy has a hard time getting the pill back up to the front of its mouth. After taking the pill, give the animal a treat to help clear the taste from its mouth.

Force-Feeding

Sometimes an animal will go off its feed, either because of mouth problems or sickness. At this time, force-feeding is necessary. The technique is similar to giving liquid medicine.

I will get some baby food, the finely processed variety that includes only veggies and water, and add some pellet powder and water. I use a 3cc syringe and give as many syringes full as the cavy will accept. I'll then fill the syringe with water and feed it to the animal.

This whole process should be repeated every couple of hours until the pig starts eating on its own again. I also try to find regular feces or cecals and force-feed them as well. While the normal feces isn't as full of B vitamins, it often contains some probiotics that can help the pig's digestive system get started again.

Hopefully, the pig will start eating on its own in a couple of days. Some antibiotics seem to upset the cavy's digestive system. One way to counter this reaction involves giving the cavy yogurt about an hour after the antibiotic. This act replaces some of the germ positive bacteria that most antibiotics seem to kill thus helping the digestive system restore itself.

Chapter Eight

Travel

Traveling with a cavy can be an adventure or a disaster, depending on how well you prepare for it. Cavies do not like new places, and they do not like motion, so traveling is very stressful for them. You can make it less stressful by doing some very simple things. First of all, get a small cat carrier that hasn't been used by a cat. Line it with towels and a t-shirt that has your scent on it. The towels help to protect the little one from bumps that might be encountered during the trip, and the shirt offers a bit of comfort to the pig by giving it a familiar smell.

When I travel, I usually put the air conditioner on, because it dries and cools the air. I try to counter this drying effect by drinking a fair amount of fluid. I help the guinea pig deal with the dry air by providing plenty of fresh produce that contains a lot of water. I also like to include some hay for it to munch on. Pellets aren't advisable during travel, because they tend to spill out of the bowl. However, hay gives the cavy something to chew. Water bottles are a definite no-no. The constant bumping causes water to spill all over the carrier. It's a good idea to save the water bottle for the rest stop.

It is important to make frequent stops and give your animal some time when the world isn't in a state of constant motion and noise. During the stops, try to cuddle your cavy (in a nice shady spot) and offer drinks from the water bottle. You can also use this opportunity to provide a handful of pellets or refresh the hay.

During travel you should take along the following items from home: a jug of water, pellets, veggies and hay. You want your animal's environment to be as much like home as possible, because you want to minimize system upsets and make the cavy a happier traveler. If you have the room, take along the cage. When you get to the motel or your destination, the cavy can move back into its home. It may have slightly different smells and sounds around it, but it will feel like home. Make sure that the motel/hotel you are staying at welcomes animals, and make every effort to minimize the extra cleaning needed due to your pet. If you want to let the cavy have some exercise time, consider taking along one of the play areas that were mentioned earlier. Fencing and a vinyl tablecloth from home may take up a little more space, but they can ensure that your cavy doesn't pick up any germs or leave any behind in the motel room.

Never leave a cavy in a car—no matter how short the—with the windows all closed and the car sitting in the sun. Cars can heat up to well over 140°F in just a few minutes. Park in the shade, leave the windows open a little bit, and if possible, leave a person with the animal to ensure its safety.

Airline travel can be very stressful for a cavy. There are only a couple of airlines that allow animals in the cabin, and the cavies have to fit in an under-seat type carrier. You should check with the airline well in advance of travel, confirm the arrangements and be ready to pay extra to have your animal travel with you. Don't be surprised if the agent at the gate seems to have a different understanding of the rules than the person you spoke with on the phone. As the public has become more concerned with animal safety, the airlines have become more sensitive to this concern.

Cargo carrying should be the last resort, and only used if you cannot avoid it. If you must send the animal by cargo, have the animal placed there as late as possible and retrieve it as quickly as possible. The cargo area isn't as comfortable as the cabin and can present your little one with many stressful situations. To make travel as comfortable as possible, purchase an airline-approved carrier, make sure the carrier has plenty of padding and fresh veggies for the trip and include something with your scent on it. Several breeders I know have sent many animals via *Delta Dash*. This service seems to handle the animals very well and have an excellent track record —they have shipped many animals across country without a single loss.

Some people take their cavies with them on camping trips. This activity has a considerable number of dangers associated with it (wild animals being the principle one), but can also give you some interesting stories to share with friends about your cavy's adventures in the great outdoors. As always, you have to be the judge of what you feel are appropriate or inappropriate activities for your animal. Remember, only do activities that are safe for your animal.

If you do take a cavy with you on a camping trip, consider how to best protect it from harm while you are sleeping. While most wild animals will steer clear of humans, there are some predators that have become used to human presence, and therefore, might enter your campsite for a snack. Make sure the snack isn't your little cavy! Take along a cage that can be closed from all sides and is difficult to open. If possible, take along a small lock that can lock the top of the cage to the side so that it cannot be opened without a key. This precaution should provide your little one with plenty of protection.

If you are visiting other people who have cavies, try to ensure that the animals you are visiting are healthy and that your animal is healthy too. Nothing can ruin a good visit and friendship like passing diseases from one animal to another. If you aren't sure about the health status of the other animals, keep your animal in the motel room. Better to scare the maid—just leave her a bigger tip—than endanger your cavy.

Chapter Nine

Other Pets

Many guinea pigs are not the only pets in the household. They often have to share a home with many different kinds of animals, and some of these animals can be dangerous to the cavy's health.

Cats

First of all, I am not a cat person by any means, and I wasn't one before I had guinea pigs. Cats are the most predatory of the domestic animals, and they will often hunt, even though they do not need to eat. This predation is one of the major causes of the decline in the songbird population in the United States (okay, off my soap box.).

Cats can, and sometimes do, live in harmony with cavies. If the cat is introduced to an adult cavy when it is a kitten, the cat is often smaller than the guinea pig and may gain a healthy respect for the cavy that will continue into adulthood. An adult cat can also be respectful of cavies, but this task is harder to manage. The initial interaction should be very controlled, preferably with the cavy safely in its cage and the cat held or harnessed in some way. Any predatory action by the cat should be discouraged immediately. Some folks use a water gun or spray bottle for controlling the cat's interactions. At no time should a cat be trusted with a guinea pig at least not until a non-predatory relationship can be established. A cat should never be left alone with a guinea pig, no matter how good a buddy the cat is.

As part of this control, the cavy's cage should have a closed top that is secured in some manner. Most of the manufactured cages offer a top that is held in place by a pair of hooks that connect to the top wire of the "front" of the cage. This safety feature should be adequate to keep the cat out. Other cages have top or front opening doors that have a latch, just make sure the cat isn't able to figure out how to open the cage.

Dogs

Dogs and cavies can get along, depending on the breed and temperament of the dog. Naturally, the "vermin hunters," like the rat terrier or any other small terrier, are not going to get along with a cavy, because they were bred to hunt such small animals. However, retrievers and other such breeds may get along well with cavies. In fact, shepherding breeds can actually be helpful if you have a small herd of cavies. Now wouldn't that be an interesting sight—a border collie controlling a herd of cavies! However, within any group there are individual differences. I have one Chihuahua that goes totally bonkers when the pigs move around in their cages. He barks and dances on his hind legs. Another Chihuahua that has visited us on occasions is totally oblivious to the pigs, while my Boxer is curious, but very gentle with the cavies.

The same rules discussed for cats apply—the interaction between dogs and cavies must begin in a very controlled environment. The dog should be put in a "down-stay" and be on a leash. The guinea pig can be introduced to the dog, while you are holding the cavy close to your body. Be prepared for the cavy to attempt to escape—after all, that is a very big predator you are introducing it to and the dog has very big teeth. Watch the dog for any signs of aggression or predatory behavior. If the dog is very well mannered, you may try putting the cavy on the floor, while controlling the dog with commands and a leash. If the dog shows any signs of attempting to hunt the cavy, return to the down-stay interaction. Naturally, I am assuming that the dog is well trained. If the dog is not well trained, you might have to consider muzzling it or keeping it totally out of the guinea pig's area.

If you move the animals to a different space or new environment, this action can create many challenges for dogs and guinea pigs. For example, if you take the cavies outside for a little bit of lawn grazing, be prepared for the dog to react in a totally different way than it did inside the house. New environments are often triggers for new behaviors on the part of the dog. If you move to a new home, the dog will have to relearn many of its behaviors. After all, this house is not "home" until you and the dog have established it as such. The dog's identification with you may be fine, but its identification with the guinea pigs may not be.

If the dog will respect it, then water gun training can also be used in this situation. However, very few dogs are intimidated by a little bit of water, so using a leash is a better option for keeping the dog under control until you are sure of its reaction to the guinea pigs.

Other Critters

Rabbits and guinea pigs have similar characteristics, and they have been known to live in reasonable harmony together. This fact does not mean that they can share a cage, but they can share playtime. Because neither animal is a predator, the interaction is based more on territorial or gender issues than on prey/predator issues. Remember, the strong hind legs of a rabbit can represent a danger to your guinea pig, so be careful with the introduction and interaction. Both of these animals have similar diets, so providing them with identical treats—romaine or pieces of carrot—can allow for positive interaction and socialization. As a cautionary note, there are diseases that rabbits carry, and are pretty much immune to, that can be fatal to a cavy. So this match up needs to be considered very carefully.

Hamsters, gerbils, ferrets and other such mammals should be handled with great care. Some diseases can be transmitted between the species. Some stories indicate that small omnivorous mammals can be a threat to the guinea pig because of their nipping and biting. A long chat with your veterinarian may be the best idea before placing your cavies near these animals.

Reptiles, especially large snakes, should not be associated with guinea pigs because the little ones would make a very nice meal for predatory lizards and snakes.

Other Guinea Pigs

Guinea pigs are very social animals, so having more than one guinea pig can increase the possibility of positive interaction. However, even this situation must be handled with great care. A female who is very territorial will not accept another female into her domain. I've even met a few females who refuse to allow a male into their domain. A male generally does not accept other males, and often tries to drive them out of its territory. Some owners put two pigs in cages that sit next to each other. This action often causes the two guinea pigs to gnaw on the bars in order to get at each other. Some people think this behavior is due to loneliness, but it can also mean that the cavies want to fight. So if you have two animals that tend to fight when put together, keep their cages a good distance apart. Sometimes close proximity can frustrate them and lead to broken teeth.

Male and female pairs often make very good matches, but one or both animals should be neutered. A severe guinea pig overpopulation problem already exists, due to the "piggie mills" that supply under-aged pigs to the pet shops, which often don't keep the sexes apart and send many sows home pregnant. Once the babies are born, they are often returned to the pet store where they start the cycle again or go to shelters that do not have the facilities or knowledge to properly care for them. Some shelters put down guinea pigs in two weeks if they are not adopted.

If you already have a cavy and want to add another to the household, there are some things that can help you accomplish this feat. Usually a younger animal can be introduced with minimal problems. Babies do well adjusting to new situations and can become close to an older, more parental pig. However, it is a good idea to keep the new pig isolated for two weeks before introducing it to another guinea pig, because it may have some medical problems. After the two weeks is up, you should try bathing both pigs, cleaning the cage and deodorizing it as best you can, and then placing both animals in the cage with a pile of vegetables. This process gives minimum "stranger scent" to the original cavy and allows the both cavies an opportunity to interact in a non-threatening manner. This single event may be all that is needed to gain acceptance. Sometimes, however, it is necessary to have several excursions to unknown territories in order to create a bond. Remember to be patient. It can work out, but in case it doesn't, be ready with a separate cage.

If the older pig attacks the younger pig, be ready to remove the baby, guarding your own well-being while doing so. Often a female will challenge, but not harm a new pig. She may chase the baby around the cage and nip at it, but she will rarely draw blood. Males, on the other hand, can be quite violent in their fights. If you observe nipping, chasing and mounting, then it isn't a problem. However, if you see the older male aim for the younger male's neck, then get the baby out quickly before he is killed. On rare occasions, you will have a female who is aggressive. If that's the case, remove the new cavy to protect her from the aggressor.

With all that said, I have successfully introduced two adult males to each other with very little dominance activity and no biting. In one case, Mishka, the existing member of my herd, was a very mellow boar. He was the best cuddler and had a very mild disposition. Badly treated in his previous home, Shadow, the new boar, was too abused to put up much of a fight. He also has a mellow personality. After a few mountings to display his authority, Mishka became very protective of Shadow. I often saw them laying next to each other, with Mishka closest to the front, protecting his weaker companion.

One of the great joys of having cavies is seeing them get along with each other after they have lived together for a while. Although they can be quite violent and dangerous, they can also be very caring and supportive. The dominant pig is often protective of the submissive pig and the cavies often groom each other and interact in other ways. As mentioned before, during exercise time, they will call to each other and make sure their partner is still around. One of my boars often called his "mate" during floor time, and she responded to him by coming out of whatever hideout she had been in and responding with a call of her own. After she passed away and he found something with her scent on it, he would still call to her.

Chapter Ten

Senior Citizens

If you have been caring for your animal well, you should end up with a senior citizen pig. Unfortunately, with old age comes a new class of concerns. Hopefully, most of these concerns will not be major.

First, you have to consider that the cavy is not going to maintain a solid adult weight. Often senior pigs tend to get a bit skinny, just as many human seniors do. While they will continue to eat well, they aren't processing the food as efficiently. To deal with this weight loss, you need to compensate by taking a couple of steps to assist their systems' operations. Give some probiotics to ensure that the cecum is properly populated, provide some Brewer's Yeast to help supplement the B vitamins, increase the vitamin C intake to help ensure that their systems are getting enough for basic needs and operations, and offer foods with a higher calcium and vitamin D content to ensure strong bones during the aging process. Each of these steps can help the cavy's body handle food more efficiently and make up for losses due to age.

Watch for signs of distress. Older cavies tend to have trouble walking or chewing. Check the eyes for any signs of infection or cataracts. While these ailments can cause blindness, most pigs do not seem to have a problem being blind. They use their nose and ears better than their eyes anyway. You should watch for signs of poor tooth condition. Their teeth often become loose and malocclusion tends to set in. These conditions lead to chewing problems.

Ultimately, you may have to make the hard decision that all pet owners have to make—do I put my animal to sleep? A basic rule of thumb for this decision is—are the times when life is good for the animal less frequent than the times when life is bad? If the answer is yes, then it is time to seriously consider taking your animal to the vet for its final visit. You are actually doing the animal a favor by removing it from a situation where the most common companion in life is pain.

Thankfully, in many cases, the animal will pass quietly in its sleep. This may be a shock to you, but it is certainly better for the animal to pass this way. As long as the animal's quality of life is good, euthanasia should not be considered. Senior pigs often make the best cuddlers—they are more mellow and less apt to be startled by noises or movement.

Another matter you should consider when you are going to put an animal to sleep is his or her companion. If the pig has lived with another pig for a long time, it can be very stressful for the survivor. During this time, watch the survivor for signs of depression and anorexia. You might even want to consider getting the lonely pig a new companion. This act will put you back into the young pig world (with all its joys) and you might find your older pig finding a renewed joy, as well. However, be prepared for the possibility that the older pig will not welcome the newcomer. As with many human pairs, the surviving member will often follow the companion into death within a short time. Do your best to ensure a quality life, but be prepared. When one of my guinea pigs, Manda Mae, passed away in her sleep, I introduced two younger females into the cage with her life mate, Spazz. He seemed to perk up for a while with the new girls, but he passed away about six weeks after Manda.

Finally, be prepared for grief. Many people think that we only grieve for other humans. I have found that this is not the case. We grieve for any being that has touched our lives in a meaningful way. Some people find it acceptable to grieve for a dog or cat, but not for rabbits or other small pets. For the life of me, I cannot understand them. When I lost each of my guinea pigs, whether I'd had it for a year or seven, I was deeply stricken. I openly wept for each one. If you are a member of a group that also cares for small animals, you will often receive sympathy notes. I have kept these notes in files as a memorial to the animals that have touched my life.

Grieve for your little darling. Let the tears fall, and then, when the time is right, find yourself another little cavy to give your love to. It is always worth it.

Chapter 11

Selecting a Healthy Guinea Pig

Buying a pet guinea pig should not include illness or pregnancy, but too often this is the case. The staff in a pet store is usually not trained to care for these animals, they are there to perform a job, not necessarily to love the animals. So here are some helpful tips to minimize your chances of having major health issues from the start.

If possible, avoid pet stores all together and try to contact a breeder. The ACBA website included in the Resources section provides a listing of member breeders. While being a member of the ACBA doesn't guarantee that the animals are well cared for, it does give you a good starting point. If you find a breeder near you, ask to visit and caviary—most good breeders love to show off their facilities and answer any questions potential buyers might have.

The first thing you should look for in a healthy cavy is its general appearance. The animal should appear to be active and in good health. The cavy should be aware and wary of your presence without showing undue fear. A cavy that doesn't run from a predator may be sick in ways that are not obvious to the untrained eye. Curiosity should be considered a good trait, because it indicates an animal that has learned humans are not to be feared.

The coat should have a nice shine and texture to it. There should be no signs of dryness or brittleness. The coat should be full and completely cover the animal, except for the top of the ears, a small area behind the ears and an area on the inside of the front feet. The coat on the belly should be as full and healthy looking as the coat on top. Check the coat for any signs of "walking dandruff," which would indicate lice. This check can be done by rubbing the coat in the wrong direction and watching near the base of the hair. Lice are most easily found on the lower back and on the neck between the ears. Its also important to check the underlying skin for any signs of redness, irritation, dryness or other skin problems. Inspect the animal for any signs of bites under the coat.

The eyes should be clear and bright with no discharge or build up of "gunk" around the edges. There should be no signs of any injuries or infection; such signs would include cloudiness or irritation around the eyes. The eyes should be round but not protrude too much from the face. The eyes should not be watery or teary.

The nose should be clear and clean with no signs of any discharge. If there is a discharge, check the color. A clear or white discharge could indicate allergies or a reaction to dust, while a yellow or green discharge could indicate a possible upper respiratory infection. Both conditions would be of concern, however, the latter is of immediate concern. Allergies are a longer term consideration.

The ears should be soft and supple. There should be little or no dry skin on the outside of the ear and no waxy buildup on the inside of the ear. The animal should not be scratching its ears on a frequent basis. Scratching with interior waxiness is often a sign of ear mites. Dry skin on the ears may indicate poor skin condition elsewhere. Go back and check the body again. Check the ears for bites. There could have been fights or aggressive mating, but either way, it suggests crowded or otherwise poor living conditions.

The feet should be clean and the pads should be soft and supple. There should be four toes on the front feet and three toes on the rear feet. Extra toes may indicate possible inbreeding and potential problems in the future. Nails should be well formed, have a sharp point and be parallel with each other (no bending off to the inside). The outside toenail on the front foot will sometimes curve under, but this should not be too obvious or impede walking.

The abdomen should be firm, but not fat. The entire body should feel solid without feeling bloated. The body should be covered with muscle. You should not be able to feel the ribs or any significant amount of bones, except in places where you would expect protrusions, such as the elbows.

If the cavy is a sow, you should feel along the sides to see if any little masses are present. A young sow can safely have a litter with proper care, but this process does tend to retard her growth and increases the chances of complications. If sows and boars are caged together, there is a very good chance of a pregnancy. Usually the sexes are separated at about three to four weeks, however, careless breeders, distributors and pet store employees often introduce males to females, leading to unwanted pregnancies.

The rump and genital area should be dry with no signs of urine scald (loss of hair and irritated skin). There should be no signs of any feces on the rump or in the fur. A case of diarrhea is a sure sign of a sick animal. The genital area should be free of any signs of discharge or irritation. You want the animal to present its underside unwillingly–no cavy ever wants to be turned upside down. While looking at the underside, make sure that the stomach is covered with a good coat of fur and there are no skin irritations or bites. In a young pup, the navel may still show as a bump, but you should look for show any signs of irritation or infection. Both boars and sows should have a pair of nipples, these should not show any sign of swelling or irritation.

During most of this inspection process, you should expect the guinea pig to protest the entire time. You would expect some shrill whistling and other sounds, possibly some tooth chattering. Listen for any raspiness or weakness in the voice. Listen to the side of the animal right over the rib cage. You should be able to hear rapid breathing, but there should be no bubbling or clicking in the breathing.

Smell the cavies. They should have a slightly musky smell that is not unpleasant. Any ammonia, feces or mildew smell would indicate either improper care or sickness. Check the cage and look for signs of poor care–if the cage isn't clean, if there is no food or water, if the water is contaminated with algae or waste or if you can see large piles of feces–then the animal has been living in unsatisfactory conditions. Consider the health of the animal under those circumstances and decide for yourself whether you can improve its health with better care.

Whatever you do, do not buy an animal to rescue it. You are simply encouraging the bad situation. Some stores actually depend on people feeling sorry for the animals and buying them under those conditions but I recommend that you don't. Instead, go to the animal control officer of that town, talk to friends and neighbors about the conditions at the store and go to the newspapers and television stations that serve that town and work to get the store closed. This activism is how you can really help the poor animals. If an animal's life is clearly in danger, make a big fuss in the store and demand that they surrender the animal to you immediately–without charge–and take it to your veterinarian. Hopefully, your vet will be able to treat the animal and file an animal abuse report against the store.

Appendix A
Guinea Pig Breeds

First of all, most of the animals you will find in a pet shop are not going to be purebred pigs. They will often be a mixture of the recognized breeds. With that said, the American Cavy Breeders Association (ACBA) recognizes thirteen breeds. In addition to the breeds, there are also many varieties within each breed. Cavies that have all the same color are called "Selfs." For example, if you have a Self Black, your animal is all black. You can also have a "TSW" meaning "tortoiseshell and white," which is a combination of black, brown and white. There are also roans in many colors, as well as Dalmatians and Himalayans. Add to these variations, the fact that many of the breeds also come in a "satin," which is considered a separate breed entirely and these breeds can become very confusing.

Breeds
American (American Satin)

The American is the standard shorthaired breed. All wild cavies and most "mutts" are American. These cavies have short hairs over their entire body. The hair is not particularly course and these animals shouldn't have any stray long hairs.

Abyssinian (Abyssinian Satin)

The Abyssinian, or Aby, breed is known as the "bad hair day" pig. Their entire body is covered with rosettes, which create swirls and ridges all over the body. They also have a wonderful "muttonchops" effect on their faces. They are too cute by half and often have a feisty attitude to go with their wild look.

Teddy (Teddy Satin)

The Teddy looks very much like a live teddy bear (hence the name). Their coats are made up of medium length hair, with a nice kink to it. Even the whiskers are kinky. In Europe there is another breed called the Rex, which looks very similar to the Teddy, but has a different genetic structure. Teddies tend to be fairly mellow pigs and should be petted "backwards" for best coat effect.

Crested

The Crested breed is actually comprised of two breeds. First, there is the Crested, which has a crest the same color as the body (also called a Self Crested). The other breed is the American Crested, which has a white crest with a body of another color. The White Crested is one of the most difficult to get right, so many babies end up either sold to pet shops or culled.

Peruvian (Peruvian Satin)

The Peruvians are wonderful animals, but very difficult to care for. They have a long coat that covers every inch of their bodies with a part down the spine. The coat has a "frontlet" which covers the face so that it is hard to tell which end is going in which direction. Without proper care, the coat can become matted and soaked with urine. However, a properly cared for Peruvian is a beautiful animal to see. Many Peruvians have very mellow personalities.

Silkie (Silkie Satin)

Silkies, or Shelties in Europe and Australia, are like Peruvians in that they have long coats, but the coat sweeps off the face, which is shorthaired like an American. These animals are also difficult to care for, but they are wonderful to see when properly done. Silkies usually have very sweet dispositions and love to be petted.

Coronet

The Coronet is a cross between the Silkie and the Crested. This breed has a lovely long coat over the rump and a crest that sprays over the face and ears. These animals have a great look to them, but they are also a very difficult breed to care for.

Texel

The Texel is a cross between a Rex and a Silkie. This breed has the long coat of a Silkie, but the curly coat is extremely difficult to keep detangled, since it wants to tangle naturally. These animals require hand washing, hand cleaning and hand drying. Fortunately, they usually have a wonderful disposition, which allows all of this work to be done to them.

Varieties
Broken

The broken variety has spots of color against a white background. These colors include all of the self colors, including agouti. Many cavies are of this variety.

Roan

Roan, like the roan in a horse, includes a white body with hairs of the roan color scattered throughout the body. Black is fairly common, but an orange or other self color is also possible. These pigs often have a face that is the roan color. Mating two roans is discouraged because it usually leads to what is called a "lethal white," a baby that is white, poorly formed, often blind, toothless and usually dies within days of birth.

Brindle

Brindle, similar to many breeds of dogs, includes a light color background with a dark banding in various widths of stripes. The most common varieties includes a honey-colored brown with black bands.

Dutch

Dutch cavies are like Dutch rabbits, they have a white band around the shoulders and a white blaze between the eyes. The body color can include any of the self colors, although black, chocolate and grey seem to be the most common.

Dalmatian

Just like the dog, a Dalmatian pig is white with clearly defined spots of color. The entire face of this variety is usually the same color as the spot color. It is very difficult to breed true since two Dalmatians will cause what is called a "lethal white" offspring.

Himalayan

The Himalayan is just like the rabbit, it has spots of color on the nose and toes with a white body. The most common spot colors are black and chocolate.

Appendix B
Breeding, An Opinion

Many folks, after having the adorable little cavy in their home for a while, think that it would be fun to breed them, just once. I strongly recommend against it! Breeding is not something that should be taken lightly, regardless of the animal involved. I have spent considerable time as a volunteer and as an adoption counselor at the Connecticut Humane Society. We have many animals that are abandoned (or surrendered if you like), including guinea pigs.

While there are areas of the country that have a shortage of cavies, most areas have an overabundance. Many of these animals end up in shelters where they are eventually destroyed. Some shelters will not accept cavies as surrendered animals and will simply put them down if found. Others will accept the animals, but have a short "shelf life" of two to three weeks. At the Connecticut Humane Society it usually takes several months for a guinea pig to be adopted.

Breeding is not a good way to make money either, unless you are going to do it the way a puppy mill does it—with inadequate diet and care and early shipping to market. If you are providing your animals with proper care, you will lose money. Responsible breeders also learn more than the minimum about the animal they are raising. This information includes medical issues, genetics, diet and a whole host of other topics.

Add to the previous reasons the very real possibility of problems arising from the breeding process. Guinea pigs have been known to suffer from pregnancy toxemia, prolapsed uterus, stillbirths, early death due to defects and other conditions that will break your heart. Yes, the babies are very cute when they survive, but they can also be very delicate and fragile.

The only reason for breeding any animal, in my mind at any rate, is to help improve the breed. This requires a level of commitment that most people are not interested in providing. It is one thing to clean a cage or two every three days, but it is an entirely different thing to do so for 20 cages. The feeding, watering, cleaning and other chores associated with even a moderate herd can quickly overwhelm many people. My herd of 8 (which includes rescues) requires a minimum of two hours every night for minimum care. The ability to provide love and ensure good health clearly suffers if you are not willing to go that extra distance.

Most of the breeders are also exhibitors. They raise the animals to compete in show competitions. This means not only raising the animals, but also caring for them and showing them. The 4-H and ACBA have programs for breeding and showing cavies. While the criteria for competition is different for the two organizations, they both believe that the animal must be in top health and a good representative of the breed. This factor adds time and cost to the process. Is it fun? Yes, it can be a lot of fun, but again it requires a considerable commitment of time and money.

For most people, the best thing to do is not to breed and simply enjoy their little pet. It might also be fun to get involved as a volunteer at your local Humane Society or shelter and see if you can help care for the guinea pigs that do come in. Very often, these shelters know plenty about dogs and cats, but very little about guinea pigs.

Glossary

Bedding: Any material used to cover the floor of a cavy's cage. It usually includes wood shavings or materials with a similar consistency.

Breeder: A person who breeds guinea pigs. There are several classes of breeders, ranging from those individuals who breed in order to improve the breed and seek to create an animal that meets the breed standard to those individuals who raise cavies as a means of making money without concern for health, temperament or well-being.

Boar: Male of the species.

Cavy: The proper name for a guinea pig.

Caviary: Usually used to describe the area where cavies live. This area can include a single large area, a room or a whole building. It is also often referred to as a stud amongst breeders.

Cecal Feces (Cecals): The soft, dark and smelly feces that is eliminated by the guinea pig. It contains much-needed B vitamins and amino acids. People rarely see cecal feces because the cavy usually ingests them directly from the anus.

Chubble: This sound is a mixture of a purr and chuckle. Some cavies make this sound and some do not. It is usually considered to be a happy sound.

Enteritis: A disorder in which the digestive system develops a gas blockage. It can be fatal if not handled promptly.

Fancier: A person who enjoys having a guinea pig or guinea pigs. The interest of these individuals usually goes beyond the simple owning of guinea pigs and includes a desire to learn as much as possible about them and their care. Generally, fanciers do not breed cavies, they simply enjoy them.

Force-feeding: When a cavy will not eat on its own volition, it must be force fed. This activity involves pushing food into the cavy's mouth with a syringe or eyedropper. It normally becomes necessary to force fluids as well

Hackles: The hair located on the shoulders of a cavy's back. These hairs are raised during male dominance fights to give cavies a larger appearance to their adversary.

Hay Rack: An open structure that hangs on the side of the cage and holds the hay. This rack is intended to keep the hay cleaner and reduce wasted hay.

Herbivore: An animal that eats only plant matter.

Hideout: Any kind of shelter that provides the cavy a place to hide. This shelter can be a box, a wooden house or even a hay rack.

Impaction: This condition can refer to two conditions. First when debris from the cage gets caught in the anus a blockage can occur. This situation usually only happens to boars because they have a scent gland in the anus which produces a sticky smelly substance that causes them to pick up debris when they drag the gland to mark their territory. Second when the anus muscles become weak and can no longer push out the cecal feces, a cecal mass forms, creating a blockage. Both kinds of impaction need to be dealt with quickly in order to ensure the safety of the animal's health.

Malocclusion: A condition in which the teeth are formed improperly from birth or become misaligned due to disease or dietary faults. The teeth grow in an irregular manner causing eating difficulties. This condition can trap the tongue, lead to starvation or cause death if not treated properly.

Mites: Small blood sucking insects that live under the skin of the cavy. During stressful periods in a cavy's life (pregnancy or sickness) mites have a better chance of overcoming an animal's natural defenses, causing additional health problems.

Motorboating: The combination of a low-pitched purr and a side-to-side strut. This combination of sound and movement usually represents the male's courting dance, but it can also be seen in dominant females and females in heat.

Pea Eye: A condition in which a portion of the eyelid protrudes. It is usually considered harmless, however, it can become a location for debris to get trapped, leading to more serious eye problems.

Pellet: A guinea pig food that is formed from long round extrusions of an alfalfa mixture, which are broken into short lengths of pelleted morsels.

Percolating: A sound made by guinea pigs when they are exploring. It sounds a bit like a "pop pop" sound, indicating that all is well with that particular cavy. It is not uncommon for another pig to call out to the percolating pig if it stops making this sound, presumably to check on its well-being.

Popcorn: During this activity, which looks like a seizure, a guinea pig runs madly around, leaps into the air twitching and squeaking, then lands and continues to run madly about. It is actually a sign of happiness and joy. It is usually seen more often in young pigs, but some adults have been known to do it as well.

Probiotics: Various germ positive bacteria that aid in the digestive process. These bacteria include acidophilus and a variety of streptococcus.

Pup: Commonly used term for the baby guinea pig.

Quick: This is a blood vessel that extends into the nail. It supplies blood to the nail, helping the nails to grow. If this vessel is nicked during nail trimming, the animal will usually cry out and the nail will bleed. If bleeding occurs, owners can simply apply pressure for a minute or so or use cornstarch or flour to aid the coagulation process. *Quik Stop* can also be used, but it stings and can cause the animal to fight all efforts to stop the bleeding.

Rumblestrutting: See Motorboating.

Salt Lick: A wheel made of salt; some are also made with additional trace minerals. If the cavy is being fed a good quality pellet then there is no need for a salt lick.

Scurvy: A disease caused by vitamin C deficiency. Signs of the disease include stiff joints, dull coat and eyes, listlessness or paralysis. The guinea pig, man and primates are the only species that do not produce their own vitamin C, and so the cavy's diet must have supplements in the form of pellets or vitamin C rich foods.

Sow: Female of the species.

Strut: When a boar is courting, he will walk in a very distinct way—very slowly with a side-to-side movement usually accompanied by a deep motorboating purr. This combination is also referred to as the rumblestrut.

Stud: See Caviary.

Urine Scald: An irritation of the skin, often accompanied by hair loss, that is caused by a cavy sitting in its own urine. Causes for this condition range from being in a poorly maintained cage to having a serious illness in which the animal has lost control of its bladder function or has become disinterested in self-preservation. Whatever the cause, it should be considered a serious problem.

Wheek: A unique sound, reserved for humans. It represents the cavy's call to its human requesting food or treats.

Resources

Books

Collins Family Pet Guide: Guinea Pigs by Peter Gurney. This new book is excellent, but shorter than the below volume by the same author. It contains much information about proper care, feed, pregnancy and other important topics. I would read this one first and then proceed to the below resource.

Diseases of the Domestic Guinea Pig by V. C. G. Richardson. The author raises guinea pigs so her knowledge of these animals is very extensive. The only possible problem with this book is that most of the treatments are listed under United Kingdom brand names, so you will have to talk to your vet about the American equivalents. This resource is an excellent book for the serious fancier. *Note:* This book has recently been revised and a 2000 edition is currently available.

The Proper Care of Guinea Pigs by Peter Gurney. This book is the best all-around book on guinea pig care. The author covers all aspects of guinea pig care and feeding. The medical information is excellent and the photographs are outstanding. Unfortunately, the publisher hasn't updated this book in seven years and it can be difficult to find in hard cover. It has recently been re-released in the UK in paperback. Check the Winkin' Cavy Store site for availability.

Your Guinea Pig: A Kids Guide to Raising and Showing by Wanda Curran. This book is aimed at the 4-H child, but it provides excellent information about the guinea pig, especially tips and strategies for breeding and showing this wonderful animal. The author also includes a list of emergency medical supplies that owners should consider having on hand.

Websites

http://acba.osb-land.com/–The American Cavy Breeders Association (ACBA) site. Besides having a listing of all members who breed guinea pigs, this site also contains discussion boards and chat areas where interested individuals can contact knowledgeable people and discuss important topics.

http://www.americanpetdiner.com–The American Pet Diner site. This site provides information about purchasing premium hays and other cavy products. They use a stabilized form of vitamin C in their cavy pellets, and offer timothy-based pellets for the bladder stone prone cavy. APD is located in Nevada.

http://www.ansci.cornell.edu/plants/alpharest.html–The Cornell Poisonous Plant Page.

http://www.geocities.com/heartland/plains/2517/–Dale Sigler's Cavy Care site; it can also be reached using *http://www.geocities.com/coachsig*. The site contains information on general care, some advanced care issues, a list of materials needed for a medical kit, silly entries from readers of the GPDD, and a link to the Rainbow Bridge site where owners can leave tributes to their departed pets.

http://go.to/gpdd–The Guinea Pig Daily Digest site. You can also go to:

http://gppd.org for the newest digest site. This is the home site for one of the longest running mailing lists on guinea pigs. The founder works at a university in Italy and has run the digest for over five years. It is a great source of general information and support.

http://www.oxbowhay.com–The Oxbow Hay Company site. This website provides information about purchasing premium hays and other cavy products for cavies. They use a stabilized form of vitamin C in their cavy pellets, and offer timothy-based pellets for the bladder stone prone cavy. Oxbow is located in Nebraska.

http://www.geocities.com/cavyrainbow/–The Rainbow Bridge site. This is a site where owners can contact the site owner and send tributes to their departed pets. Prose, poetry and photos are welled for the site.

http://www.aracnet.com/~seagull/Guinea–Seagull's site. A very good site with lots of general info and pictures of *Neat Idea Cube* uses. Special features include a table of vitamin C rich vegetables, information on pregnancy and a vet finder function based on visitor input.

http://www.nal.usda.gov/fnic/foodcomp/Data/–The USDA Database on Foods.

http://www.winking-cavy.co.uk/–The Winking Cavy Store is a United Kingdom site with all kinds of goods, books, and materials pertaining to the guinea pig. About the only real source for Peter Gurney's two books.

The following sites discuss the hazards of using cedar and raw pine shavings as bedding:
http://www.trifl.org/cedar.html
http://www.halcyon.com/integral/warning.html
http://12.16.135.156/cedarand.htm

http://www.rabbit.org/journal/1/liver-disease.html
http://www.sonic.net/~melissk/cedar.html
http://home.earthlink.net/~zoohcorner/litterliver.htm

Mailing Lists

Individuals can join the *Guinea Pig Daily Digest* (GPDD) by sending a message to: *listproc@ing.unico.it*—with the body message reading "subscribe gpigs {your name}". In a short time, they will receive a confirmation message and directions on how to use the list. The GPDD covers general care issues. It also offers various virtual events in which guinea pigs go off on adventures to different locations. This mailing list is a lot of fun, but it also privdes serious information as well.

Guinea Pig List is another mailing list that is set up as a post and respond resource. It is intended for a more rapid response to questions. This list is not for discussion of breeding (except for accidental pregnancies) or for the "silly" stuff that happens on the GPDD. The focus here is on good care and husbandry. Individuals can subscribe to it via Seagull's site mentioned above or by sending a message to: *listproc@listserver.com*—with a body message reading "subscribe guinea-pigs {your name}".

There are also several mailing lists on EGroup. Individuals can go to *http://www.egroup.com* and do a search on guinea pigs. They'll find several groups at this website and receive very easy instructions on how to subscribe to any of the selected mailing lists. The *Cavy-Lovers List* is one that I belong to.

Bibliography

The following four books should form the foundation of any good library for dedicated cavy owners. Depending on your inclination and budget, there are many other books available on various topics related to guinea pigs and their care.

Curran, Wanda L. *Your Guinea Pig: A Kid's Guide to Raising and Showing*. Pownel, VT: A Garden Way Publishing Book, 1995.

Gurney, Peter. *Guinea Pig*. London: Harper Collins Publishers, 1999.

Gurney, Peter. *The Proper Care of Guinea Pigs*. Neptune City NJ: T.F.H. Publications Inc., 1992.

Richardson, V. C. G. MA VetMB MRCVS. *Diseases of the Domestic Guinea Pig*. Oxford: Blackwell Science Ltd., 1992.

Printed in the United States
20319LVS00005B/367-369